William Cowper, John Bewick

The Children's miscellany

The history of little Jack

William Cowper, John Bewick

The Children's miscellany
The history of little Jack

ISBN/EAN: 9783337203887

Printed in Europe, USA, Canada, Australia, Japan

Cover: Foto ©Lupo / pixelio.de

More available books at **www.hansebooks.com**

THE
Children's Miscellany:

IN WHICH IS INCLUDED

THE HISTORY OF LITTLE JACK;

BY THOMAS DAY, ESQ.

AUTHOR OF THE HISTORY OF

SANDFORD AND MERTON.

Bid him, besides, his daily pains employ,
To form the tender manners of the boy;
And work him, like a waxen babe, with art,
To perfect symmetry in every part.   DRYDEN.

A NEW EDITION,

*Embellished with Twenty-eight Cuts, by Bewick,
and a Frontispiece.*

London:

PRINTED FOR JOHN STOCKDALE, PICCADILLY.

1797.

ADVERTISEMENT.

AS the Editor of this collection is conſcious there may appear ſome defects in the arrangement of his materials, he thinks it neceſſary to acquaint the Public with the true reaſon of their appearing in a leſs finiſhed ſtate than he could have wiſhed to preſent them. Some gentlemen of fortune and literary abilities had once conceived the ſcheme of contributing to the entertainment and inſtruction of the riſing generation by a ſelection of the moſt intereſting and improving hiſtories from different authors. They intended to tranſlate from the different languages of Europe

rope whatever might engage the minds of children to the improvement of their knowledge, and inspire them with an early love of virtue. To these they were to have added a judicious selection from natural history, and the most entertaining descriptions that are to be found in the ample collection of modern voyages; together with many original pieces of their own composition. All these, it was presumed, would contribute a pleasing and useful Miscellany for the use of children, which they intended to have published in periodical numbers. After they had made some progress in the execution of this scheme, they were compelled, by accidents which it is unnecessary to relate, to abandon their design. But, though the modesty of the authors would rather have led them to suppress what they could not engage to finish, the Editor, to whom their

papers

ADVERTISEMENT.

papers were entrusted, has judged them too valuable to be entirely suppressed. He has, therefore, collected them into a volume, with the hopes that this Miscellany may not appear undeserving of the public favour, and may be deemed no contemptible addition to that branch of literature which proposes to itself the important object of pleasing and instructing children.

THE HISTORY

OF

LITTLE JACK.

THERE was once a poor lame old man that lived in the midſt of a wide unculti‑vated moor, in the north of England. He had formerly been a ſoldier, and had almoſt loſt the uſe of one leg by a wound he had received in battle, when he was fighting againſt the enemies of his country. This poor man, when he found himſelf thus diſabled, built a little hut of clay, which he covered with turf dug from the com‑mon. He had a little bit of ground which he made a ſhift to cultivate with his own hands, and which ſupplied him with potatoes and ve‑getables; beſides this, he ſometimes gained a few halfpence by opening a gate for travellers, which ſtood near his houſe. He did not indeed get much, becauſe few people paſſed that way. What he earned was, however, enough to pur‑chaſe cloaths, and the few neceſſaries he want‑ed. But though poor, he was ſtrictly honeſt, and never failed night and morning to addreſs his prayers to God; by which means he was re‑ſpected by all who knew him, much more than many

many who were superior to him in rank and fortune. This old man had one domestic. In his walks over the common, he one day found a little kid that had lost its mother, and was almost famished with hunger: he took it home to his cottage, fed it with the produce of his garden, and nursed it till it grew strong and vigorous. Little Nan, (for that was the name he gave it) returned his cares with gratitude, and became as much attached to him as a dog. All day she browzed upon the herbage that grew around his hut, and at night reposed upon the same bed of straw with her master. Frequently did she divert him with her innocent tricks and gambols. She would nestle her little head in his bosom, and eat out of his hand part of his scanty allowance of bread, which he never failed to divide with his favourite. The old man often beheld her with silent joy, and, in the innocent effusions of his heart, would lift his hands to heaven, and thank the Deity, that, even in the midst of poverty and distress, had raised him up one faithful friend.

One night, in the beginning of winter, the old man thought he heard the feeble cries and lamentations of a child. As he was naturally charitable, he arose and struck a light, and, going out of his cottage, examined on every side. It was

was not long before he discerned an infant, which had probably been dropped by some strolling beggar or gypsy. The old man stood amazed at the sight, and knew not what to do. Shall I, said he, who find it so difficult to live at present, incumber myself with the care of an helpless infant, that will not for many years be capable of contributing to its own subsistence? And yet, added he, softening with pity, can I deny assistance to a human being still more miserable than myself?—Will not that Providence which feeds the birds of the wood and the beasts of the field, and which has promised to bless all those that are kind and charitable, assist my feeble endeavours?—At least, let me give it food and lodging for this night; for without I receive it into my cottage, the poor abandoned wretch must perish with cold before the morning. Saying this, he took it up in his arms, and perceived it was a fine healthy boy, though covered with rags; the little foundling too seemed to be sensible of his kindness, and smiling in his face, stretched out his little arms, as if to embrace his benefactor.

When he had brought it into his hut, he began to be extremely embarrassed how to procure it food: but looking at Nan, he recollected that she had just lost her kid, and saw her udder distended

tended with milk: he, therefore, called her to him, and, prefenting the child to the teat, was overjoyed to find, that it fucked as naturally as if it had really found a mother. The goat too feemed to receive pleafure from the efforts of

the child, and fubmitted without oppofition to difcharge the duties of a nurfe. Contented with
this

this experiment, the old man wrapped the child up as warmly as he could, and stretched himself out to rest, with the consciousness of having done a humane action. Early the next morning he was awakened by the cries of the child for food, which, with the assistance of his faithful Nan, he suckled as he had done the night before. And now the old man began to feel an interest in the child, which made him defer some time longer the taking measures to be delivered from its care. Who knows, said he, but Providence, which has preserved this child in so wonderful a manner, may have destined it to something equally wonderful in his future life, and may bless me as the humble agent of his decrees? At least, as he grows bigger, he will be a pleasure and comfort to me in this lonely cabin, and will assist in cutting turf for fuel, and cultivating the garden. From this time he became more and more attached to the little foundling; who, in a short time, learned to consider the old man as a parent, and delighted him with its innocent caresses. Gentle Nanny too, the goat, seemed to adopt him with equal tenderness as her offspring: she would stretch herself out upon the ground, while he crawled upon his hands and knees towards her; and when he had

satisfied

satisfied his hunger by sucking, he would nestle between her legs and go to sleep in her bosom.

It was wonderful to see how this child, thus left to nature, increased in strength and vigour. Unfettered by bandages or restraints, his limbs acquired their due proportions and form; his countenance was full and florid, and gave indications of perfect health; and, at an age when other children are scarcely able to support themselves with the assistance of a nurse, this little foundling could run alone. It was true that he sometimes failed in his attempts, and fell to the ground; but the ground was soft, and little Jack, for so the old man called him, was not tender or delicate; he never minded thumps or bruises; but boldly scrambled up again and pursued his way. In a short time, little Jack was completely master of his legs; and as the summer came on, he attended his mamma, the goat,

upon

upon the common, and used to play with her for hours together; sometimes rolling under her belly, now climbing upon her back, and frisking about as if he had really been a kid. As to his cloathing, Jack was not much incumbered with it: he had neither shoes, nor stockings, nor shirt; but the weather was warm, and Jack felt himself so much lighter for every kind of exercise. In a short time after this, Jack began to imitate the sounds of his papa, the man, and his mamma, the goat; nor was it long before he learned to speak articulately. The old man, delighted with this first dawn of reason, used to place him upon his knee, and converse with him for hours together, while his pottage was slowly boiling amid the embers of a turf fire. As he grew bigger, Jack became of considerable use to his father; he could trust him to look after the gate, and open it during his absence; and, as to the cookery of the family, it was not long before Jack was a complete proficient, and could make broth almost as well as his daddy himself. During the winter nights, the old man used to entertain him with stories of what he had seen during his youth; the battles and sieges he had been witness to, and the hardships he had undergone; all this he related with so much vivacity, that Jack was never tired of listening. But what de-

lighted

lighted him beyond meafure was to fee daddy fhoulder his crutch, inftead of a mufquet, and give the word of command. To the right—to the left—prefent—fire—march—halt—all this was familiar to Jack's ear as foon as he could fpeak, and before he was fix years old, he poized and prefented a broom-ftick, which his daddy gave him for that purpofe, with as good a grace as any foldier of his age in Europe.

The old man too inftructed him in fuch plain and fimple morals and religion, as he was able to explain. "Never tell an untruth, Jack," faid he, " even though you were to be flayed alive; a foldier never lies." Jack held up his head, marched acrofs the floor, and promifed his daddy that he would always tell the truth like a foldier. But the old man, as he was fomething of
a fcholar

a scholar, had a great ambition that his darling should learn to read, and write; and this was a work of some difficulty; for he had neither printed book, nor pens, nor paper in his cabin. Industry, however, enables us to overcome difficulties; in the summer time, as the old man sat before his cottage, he would draw letters in the sand, and teach Jack to name them singly, until he was acquainted with the whole alphabet, he then proceeded to syllables, and after that to words; all which his little pupil learned to pronounce with great facility: and, as he had a strong propensity to imitate what he saw, he not only acquired the power of reading words, but of tracing all the letters which composed them, on the sand.

About this time, the poor goat, which had nursed Jack so faithfully, grew ill and died. He tended her with the greatest affection and assiduity during her illness, brought her the freshest herbs for food, and would frequently support her head for hours together upon his little bosom. But it was all in vain; he lost his poor mammy, as he used to call her, and was for some time inconsolable; for Jack, though his knowledge was bounded, had an uncommon degree of gratitude and affection in his temper. He was not able to talk as finely about love, tenderness, and sensibility, as many other little boys, that have enjoyed

greater

greater advantages of education, but he felt the reality of them in his heart, and thought it so natural to love every thing that loves us, that he never even suspected it was possible to do otherwise. The poor goat was buried in the old man's garden, and thither little Jack would often come, and call upon his poor mammy Nan, and ask her why she had left him? One day, as he was thus employed, a lady happened to come by in a carriage, and overheard him before he was aware. Jack ran in an instant to open the gate; but the lady stopped, and asked him whom he was bemoaning so pitifully, and calling upon. Jack

answered, that it was his poor mammy, that was buried in the garden. The lady thought it very odd to hear of such a burial place, and therefore proceeded to question him, "How did your mamma

mamma get her living?" said she. "She used to graze here upon the common all day long," said Jack. The lady was still more astonished; but the old man came out of his hut, and explained the whole affair to her, which surprized her very much; for though this lady had seen a great deal of the world, and had read a variety of books, it had never once entered into her head that a child might grow strong and vigorous by sucking a goat, instead of eating pap. She therefore looked at Jack with amazement, admired his brown but animated face, and praised his shape and activity. "Will you go with me, little boy?" said she, "and I will take care of you, if you behave well." "No," said Jack, "I must stay with daddy; he has taken care of me for many years, and now I must take care of him; otherwise I should like very well to go with such a sweet, good-natured lady." The lady was not displeased with Jack's answer, and putting her hand in her pocket, gave him half a crown, to buy him shoes and stockings, and pursued her journey.

Jack was not unacquainted with the use of money, as he had been often sent to the next village to purchase bread and necessaries; but he was totally unacquainted with the use of shoes and stockings, which he had never worn in his life,

life, or felt the want of. The next day, however, the old man bade him run to town, and lay his money out as the lady had defired; for he had too much honour to think of difobeying her commands, or fuffering it to be expended for any other purpofe. It was not long before Jack returned; but the old man was much furprized to fee him come back as bare as he went out. " Heigh, Jack!" faid he, " where are the fhoes and ftockings which you were to purchafe?" " Daddy, anfwered Jack, " I went to the fhop, and juft tried a pair for fport, but I found them fo cumberfome, that I could not walk, and I would not wear fuch things, even if the lady would give me another half crown for doing it; fo I laid the money out in a warm jacket for you, becaufe the winter is coming on, and you feem to be more afraid of the cold than formerly." Many fuch inftances of conduct did Jack difplay; from which it was eafy to perceive, that he had an excellent foul and generous temper. One failing, indeed, Jack was liable to; though a very good natured boy, he was a little too jealous of his honour. His daddy had taught him the ufe of his hands and legs, and Jack had fuch difpofitions for the art of boxing, that he could beat every boy in the neighbourhood, of his age and fize. Even if they were a head taller,

it

it made no difference to Jack, provided they said any thing to wound his honour; for otherwife he was the moſt mild, pacific creature in the world. One day that he had been fent to the village, he returned with his eyes black, and his face fwelled to a frightful fize: it was even with difficulty that he was able to walk at all, fo fore was he with the pomelling he had received. "What have you been doing now, Jack?" faid the old man.—" Only fighting with Dick the butcher." " You rogue, faid the old man, he is twice as big as you are, and the beſt fighter in all the country." " What does that fignify, faid Jack, he called you an old beggarman, and then I ſtruck him; and I will ſtrike him again whenever he calls you fo, even if he fhould beat me to pieces; for you know daddy, that you are not a beggarman, but a foldier."

In this manner lived little Jack, until he was twelve years old; at this time his poor old daddy fell fick and became incapable of moving about. Jack did every thing he could think of for the poor man; he made him broths, he fed him with his own hands, he watched whole nights by his bed-fide fupporting his head and helping him when he wanted to move. But it was all in vain; his poor daddy grew daily worfe, and perceived it to be impoſſible that he fhould recover.

cover. He one day therefore called little Jack to his bed-fide, and preffing his hand affectionately, told him that he was juft going to die. Little Jack burft into a flood of tears at this information, but his daddy defired him to compofe himfelf, and attend to the laft advice he

fhould be able to give him. " I have lived, faid the old man, a great many years, in poverty, but I do not know that I have been worfe off than if I had been rich. I have avoided, perhaps, many faults, and many uneafineffes, which I fhould have incurred had I been in another fituation; and though I have often wanted a meal and always fared hard, I have enjoyed as much health and life as ufually falls to the lot of my betters. I am now going to die; I feel it in every part; the breath will foon be out

out of my body; then I fhall be put in the ground, and the worms will eat your poor old daddy." At this Jack renewed his tears and fobbings, for he was unable to reftrain them. But the old man faid; " Have patience, my child; though I fhould leave this world, as I have always been ftrictly honeft and endeavoured to do my duty, I do not doubt but God will pity me, and convey me to a better place; where I fhall be happier than I have ever been here. This is what I have always taught you, and this belief gives me the greateft comfort in my laft moments. The only regret I feel, is for you, my deareft child, whom I leave unprovided for. But you are ftrong and vigorous, and almoft able to get your living. As foon as I am dead, you muft go to the next village and inform the people, that they may come and bury me. You muft then endeavour to get into fervice, and work for your living; and, if you are ftrictly honeft and fober, I do not doubt that you will find a livelihood, and that God, who is the common father of all, will protect and blefs you. Adieu, my child, I grow fainter and fainter; never forget your poor old daddy, nor the example he has fet you; but in every fituation of life difcharge your duty, and live like a foldier, and a Chriftian." When the old man had with difficulty uttered thefe laft in-

ftructions,

ſtructions, his voice entirely failed him, his limbs grew cold and ſtiff, and in a few minutes he expired without a groan. Little Jack, who hung crying over his daddy, called upon him in vain, in vain endeavoured to revive him. At length he pulled off his cloaths, went into his daddy's bed, and endeavoured for many hours to animate him with the warmth of his own body; but finding all his endeavours fruitleſs, he concluded that he was indeed dead; and therefore, weeping bitterly, he dreſt himſelf, and went to the village as he had been ordered. The poor little boy was thus left entirely deſtitute and knew not what to do; but one of the farmers, who had been acquainted with him before, offered to take him into his houſe, and give him his victuals, for a few months, till he could find a ſervice. Jack thankfully accepted the offer, and ſerved him faithfully for ſeveral months; during which time he learned to milk, to drive the plough, and never refuſed any kind of work he was able to perform. But, by ill luck, this good-natured farmer contracted a fever, by over-heating himſelf in the harveſt, and died in the beginning of winter. His wife was therefore obliged to diſcharge her ſervants, and Jack was again turned looſe upon the world, with only his cloaths, and a ſhilling in his pocket, which his kind miſtreſs had made him a preſent of.

of. He was very forry for the lofs of his mafter; but he was now grown bigger and ftronger, and thought he fhould eafily find employment. He therefore fet out upon his travels, walking all day, and inquiring at every farm-houfe for work. But in this attempt he was unfortunate, for nobody chofe to employ a ftranger: and though he lived with the greateft economy, he foon found himfelf in a worfe fituation than ever, without a farthing in his pocket or a morfel of bread to eat. Jack, however, was not of a temper to be eafily caft down; he walked refolutely on all day, but towards evening was overtaken by a violent ftorm of rain, which wetted him to the fkin before he could find a bufh for fhelter. Now, poor Jack began to think of his old daddy, and the comforts he had formerly enjoyed upon the common, where he had always a roof to fhelter him, and a flice of bread for fupper. But tears and lamentations were vain; and therefore, as foon as the ftorm was over, he purfued his journey, in hopes of finding fome barn or out-houfe to creep into for the reft of the night. While he was thus wandering about, he faw at fome diftance a great light, which feemed to come from fome prodigious fire. Jack did not know what this could be; but, in his prefent fituation, he thought a fire no difagreeable object, and therefore determined to
approach

approach it. When he came nearer, he saw a large building which seemed to spout fire and smoke at several openings, and heard an incessant noise of blows, and the rattling of chains. Jack was at first a little frightened, but summoning all his courage, he crept cautiously on to the building, and looking through a chink, discovered se-

veral men and boys employed in blowing fires and hammering burning masses of iron. This was a very comfortable sight to him in his present forlorn condition; so finding a door half open, he ventured in, and placed himself as near as he dared to one of the flaming furnaces. It was not long before he was discovered by one of the workmen, who asked him, roughly, what business he had there? Jack answered, with great humility, that he was a poor boy, looking out for work;
that

that he had had no food all day, and was wet to the fkin with the rain, which was evident enough from the appearance of his cloaths. By great good luck, the man he fpoke to was good-natured, and therefore not only permitted him to ftay by the fire, but gave him fome broken victuals for his fupper. After this, he laid himfelf down in a corner, and flept without difturbance till morning. He was fcarcely awake the next day, when the mafter of the forge came in to overlook his men, who finding Jack, and hearing his ftory, began to reproach him as a lazy vagabond, and afked him why he did not work for his living. Jack affured him there was nothing he fo earneftly defired, and that if he would pleafe to employ him, there was nothing he would not do to earn a fubfiftence. Well, my boy, faid the mafter, if this is true, you fhall foon be tried; nobody need be idle here; fo calling his foreman, he ordered him to fet that lad to work, and pay him in proportion to his deferts. Jack now thought himfelf completely happy, and worked with fo much affiduity, that he foon gained a comfortable livelihood, and acquired the efteem of his mafter. But unfortunately, he was a little too unreferved in his converfation, and communicated the ftory of his former life and education. This was great matter of diverfion to all the other boys of the
forge;

forge; who, whenever they were inclined to be merry, would call him little Jack the beggar-boy, and imitate the baaing of a goat. This was too much for his irafcible temper, and he never failed to refent it; by which means he was engaged in continual quarrels and combats, to the great difturbance of the houfe; fo that his mafter, though in other refpects perfectly fatisfied with his behaviour, began to fear that he fhould at laft be obliged to difcharge him.

It happened one day, that a large company of gentlemen and ladies were introduced to fee the works. The mafter attended them, and explain-

ed, with great politenefs, every part of his manufacture. They viewed with aftonifhment the different methods by which that ufeful and neceffary ore of iron is rendered fit for human ufe. They examined

amined the furnaces where it is melted down, to
difengage it from the drofs, with which it is mixed
in the bowels of the earth, and whence it runs down
in liquid torrents like fire. They beheld with equal
pleafure the prodigious hammers, which, moved
by the force of water, mould it into maffy bars,
for the fervice of man. While they were bufy in
examining thefe different proceffes, they were
alarmed by a fudden noife of difcord, which
broke out on the other fide of the building; and
the mafter enquiring into the caufe, was told,
that it was only little Jack, who was fighting
with Tom the collier. At this, the mafter cried

out, in a paffion, there is no peace to be expected
in the furnace, while that little rafcal is employed; fend him to me, and I will inftantly difcharge him. At this moment Jack appeared,
all

all covered with blood and dirt, and ſtood before his angry judge in a modeſt, but reſolute poſture. "Is this the reward," ſaid his maſter, "you little audacious vagabond, of all my kindneſs? Can you never refrain a ſingle inſtant from broils and fighting? But I am determined to bear it no longer; and therefore you ſhall never, from this hour, do a ſingle ſtroke of work for me." "Sir," replied Jack, with great humility, but yet with firmneſs, "I am extremely ſorry to have diſobliged you, nor have I ever done it willingly ſince I have been here; and if the other boys would only mind their buſineſs as well as I do, and not moleſt me, you would not have been offended now; for I defy them all to ſay, that, ſince I have been in the houſe, I have ever given any one the leaſt provocation, or ever refuſed, to the utmoſt of my ſtrength, to do whatever I have been ordered." "That's true, in good faith," ſaid the foreman; I muſt do little Jack the juſtice to ſay, that there is not a more honeſt, ſober, and induſtrious lad about the place. Set him to what you will, he never ſculks, never grumbles, never ſlights his work; and if it were not for a little paſſion and fighting, I don't believe there would be his fellow in England." "Well," ſaid the maſter, a little mollified, "but what is the cauſe of all this ſudden diſturbance?" "Sir," anſwered ed Jack, "it is Tom that has been abusing me, and telling me that my father was a beggarman and my mother a nanny-goat; and when I desired him to be quiet, he went baaing all about the house; and this I could not bear; for as to my poor father, he was an honest soldier, and if I did suck a goat, she was the best creature in the world, and I won't hear her abused while I have any strength in my body." At this harangue, the whole audience were scarcely able to refrain from laughing, and the master, with more composure, told Jack to mind his business, and threatened the other boys with punishment if they disturbed him.

But a lady who was in company seemed particularly interested about little Jack, and when she had heard his story, said, this must certainly be the little boy who opened a gate several years past for me upon Norcot Moor. I remember being struck with his appearance, and hearing him lament the loss of the goat that nursed him. I was very much affected with his history, and since he deserves so good a character, if you will part with him, I will instantly take him into my service. The master replied, that he should part with him with great satisfaction to such an excellent mistress; that, indeed, the boy deserved all the commendations which had been given; but
since

since the other lads had such an habit of plaguing, and Jack was of so impatient a temper, he despaired of ever composing their animosities. Jack was then called, and informed of the lady's offer, which he instantly accepted with the greatest readiness, and received immediate directions to her house.

Jack was now in a new sphere of life. His face was washed, his hair combed, he was clothed afresh, and appeared a very smart active lad. His business was to help in the stable, to water the horses, to clean shoes, to perform errands, and to do all the jobs of the family; and in the discharge of these services, he soon gave universal satisfaction. He was indefatigable in doing what he was ordered, never grumbled, or appeared out of temper, and seemed so quiet and inoffensive in his manners, that every body wondered how he had acquired the character of being quarrelsome. In a short time, he became both the favourite and the drudge of the whole family; for, speak but kindly to him, and call him a little soldier, and Jack was at every one's disposal. This was Jack's particular foible and vanity; at his leisure hours, he would divert himself by the hour together in poizing a dung-fork, charging with a broomstick, and standing centry at the stable-door. Another propensity of Jack's,
which

which now difcovered itfelf, was an immoderate
love of horfes. The inftant he was introduced
into the ftable, he attached himfelf fo ftrongly
to thefe animals, that you would have taken him
for one of the fame fpecies, or at leaft a near relation. Jack was never tired with rubbing down
and currying them; the coachman had fcarcely
any bufinefs but to fit upon his box; all the ope-
rations of the ftable were intrufted to little Jack,
nor was it ever known that he neglected a fingle
particular. But what gave him more pleafure
than all the reft, was fometimes to accompany
his miftrefs upon a little horfe, which he managed with infinite dexterity.

Jack too difcovered a great difpofition for all
the ufeful and mechanic arts. He had ferved an
apprenticefhip already to the manufactory of
iron, and of this he was almoft as vain as being
a foldier. As he began to extend his knowledge
of the world, he faw that nothing could be done
without iron. How would you plough the
ground, faid Jack; how would you dig your garden; how would you even light a fire, drefs a
dinner, fhoe a horfe, or do the leaft thing in the
world, if we workmen at the forge did not take
the trouble of preparing it for you? Thus Jack
would fometimes expatiate upon the dignity and
importance of his own profeffion to the great
admiration of all the other fervants. Thefe ideas

naturally

naturally gave Jack a great esteem for the profession of a blacksmith, and in his occasional visits to the forge with the horses, he learnt to make and fix a shoe as neatly as any artist in the country. Nor were Jack's talents confined to the manufactory of iron; his love of horses was so

great, and his interest in every thing that related to them, that it was not long before he acquired a very competent knowledge in the art of sadlery.

Jack would also sometimes observe the carpenters when they were at work, and sometimes by stealth attempt the management of their tools, in which he succeeded as well as in every thing else, so that he was looked upon by every body as a very active, ingenious boy.

There was in the family where he now lived a young gentleman, the nephew of his mistress, who had lost his parents, and was therefore
brought

brought up by his aunt. As Maſter Willets was ſomething younger than Jack, and a very good-natured boy, he ſoon began to take notice of him, and be much diverted with his company. Jack, indeed, was not undeſerving this attention; for although he could not boaſt any great advantages of education, his conduct was entirely free from all the vices to which ſome of the lower claſs of people are ſubject. Jack was never heard to ſwear, or expreſs himſelf with any indecency. He was civil and reſpectful in his manners to all his ſuperiors, and uniformly good-natured to his equals. In reſpect to the animals entruſted to his care, he not only refrained from uſing them ill, but was never tired with doing them good offices. Added to this, he was ſober, temperate, hardy, active, and ingenious, and deſpiſed a lie as much as any of his betters. Maſter Willets now began to be much pleaſed with playing at cricket and trap-ball with Jack, who excelled at both theſe games. Maſter Willets had a little horſe, which Jack looked after, and not contented with looking after him in the beſt manner, he uſed to ride him at his leiſure hours with ſo much care and addreſs, that in a ſhort time he made him the moſt gentle and docile little animal in the country. Jack had acquired this knowledge partly from his own experience, and partly from paying particular attention to an

itinerant

itinerant riding-master, that had lately exhibited various feats in that neighbourhood. Jack attended him so closely, and made so good an use of his time, that he learned to imitate almost every thing he saw, and used to divert the servants and his young master with acting the taylor's riding to Brentford.

The young gentleman had a master who used to come three times a week to teach him accounts, and writing, and geography. Jack used to be sometimes in the room while the lessons were given, and listened, according to custom, with so much attention to all that passed, that he received very considerable advantage for his own improvement. He had now a little money, and he laid some of it out to purchase pens, and paper, and a slate, with which at night he used to imitate every thing he had heard and seen in

the

the day; and his little master, who began to love him very sincerely, when he saw him so desirous of improvement, contrived, under one pretence or another, to have him generally in the room while he was receiving instruction himself.

In this manner Jack went on for some years, leading a life very agreeable to himself, and discharging his duty very much to the satisfaction of his mistress. An unlucky accident at length happened to interrupt his tranquillity. A young gentleman came down to visit Master Willets, who, having been educated in France, and among genteel people in London, had a very great taste for finery, and a supreme contempt for all the vulgar. His dress too was a little particular, as well as his manners; for he spent half his time in adjusting his head, wore a large black bag tied to his hair behind, and would sometimes strut about for half an hour together with his hat un-

der

der his arm, and a little fword by his fide. This young man had a fupreme contempt for all the vulgar, which he did not attempt to conceal; and when he had heard the ftory of Jack's birth and education, he could fcarcely bear to be in the fame room with him. Jack foon perceived the averfion which the ftranger entertained for him, and at firft endeavoured to remove it, by every civility in his power; but when he found that he gained nothing by all his humility, his temper, naturally haughty, took fire, and, as far as he dared, he plainly fhewed all the refentment he felt.

It happened one day, after Jack had received fome very mortifying ufage from this young gentleman, that as he was walking along the road, he met with a fhowman, who was returning from a neighbouring fair with fome wild beafts in a cart. Among the reft was a middle-fized monkey, who was not under cover like the reft, and played fo many antic tricks, and made fo many grimaces, as engaged all Jack's attention, and delighted him very much, for he always had a propenfity for every fpecies of drollery. After a variety of queftions and converfation, the fhowman, who probably wanted to be rid of his monkey, propofed to Jack to purchafe him for half a crown. Jack could not refift the temptation of being mafter of fuch a droll diverting animal, and

therefore

therefore agreed to the bargain. But when he was left alone with his purchaſe, whom he led along by a chain, he ſoon began to repent his haſte, and knew not how to diſpoſe of him. As there was, however, no remedy, Jack brought him carefully home, and confined him ſafe in an out-houſe, which was not applied to any uſe.— In this ſituation he kept him ſeveral days, without accident, and frequently viſited him at his leiſure hours, with apples, nuts, and ſuch other preſents as he could procure. Among the other tricks which the monkey had been taught to perform, he would riſe upon his hind legs at the word of command, and bow with the greateſt politeneſs to the company. Jack, who had found out theſe accompliſhments in his friend, could not reſiſt the impulſe of making them ſubſervient to his reſentment. He, therefore, one day, procured ſome flour, with which he powdered his monkey's head, fixed a large paper bag to his neck, put an old hat under his arm, and tied a large iron ſkewer to his ſide, inſtead of a ſword; and thus accoutred, led him about with infinite ſatisfaction, calling him Monſieur, and jabbering ſuch broken French as he had picked up from the converſation of the viſitor. It happened very unluckily at this very inſtant, that the young gentleman himſelf paſſed by,

and

and inftantly faw at one glance the intended copy himfelf, and all the malice of little Jack; who was leading him along, and calling to him to hold

up his head, and look like a perfon of fafhion. Rage inftantly took poffeffion of his mind, and drawing his fword, which he happened to have on, he ran the poor monkey through with a fudden thruft, and laid him dead upon the ground. What more he might have done is uncertain, for Jack, who was not of a temper to fee calmly fuch an outrage committed upon an animal whom he confidered as his friend, flew upon him like a fury, and wrefting the fword out of his hand, broke it into twenty pieces. The young gentleman himfelf received a fall in the fcuffle, which, though it did him no material damage, daubed all his cloaths, and totally fpoiled the whole

whole arrangement of his drefs. At this inftant, the lady herfelf, who had heard the noife, came down, and the violence of poor Jack was too apparent to be excufed. Jack, indeed, was fubmiffive to his miftrefs, whom he was very forry to have offended; but, when he was ordered to make conceffions to the young gentleman, as the only conditions upon which he could be kept in the family, he abfolutely refufed. He owned, indeed, that he was much to blame for refenting the provocations he had received, and endeavouring to make his miftrefs's company ridiculous; but as to what he had done in defence of his friend the monkey, there were no poffible arguments which could convince him he was in the leaft to blame; nor would he have made fubmiffions to the King himfelf.— This unfortunate obftinacy of Jack's was the

occafion

occaſion of his being diſcharged, very much to the regret of the lady herſelf, and ſtill more to that of Maſter Willets. Jack therefore packed up his cloaths in a little bundle, ſhook all his fellow-ſervants by the hand, took an affectionate leave of his kind maſter, and once more ſallied out upon his travels.

He had not walked far before he came to a town, where a party of ſoldiers were beating up for volunteers. Jack mingled with the crowd that ſurrounded the recruiting ſerjeant, and liſtened with great pleaſure to the ſound of the fifes and drums; nor could he help mechanically holding up his head, and ſtepping forward with an air that ſhewed the trade was not entirely new to him. The ſerjeant ſoon took notice of theſe geſtures, and ſeeing him a ſtrong likely lad, came up to him, clapped him upon the

the back, and asked him if he would enlist.—
"You are a brave boy," said he, "I can see it

in your looks—come along with us, and I don't doubt, in a few weeks, you'll be as complete a soldier as those who have been in the army for years."

Jack made no answer to this, but by instantly poizing his stick, cocking his hat fiercely, and going through the whole manual exercise.—"Prodigious, indeed!" cried the serjeant, "I see you have been in the army already, and can eat fire as well as any of us. But come with us, my brave lad, you shall live well, have little to do, but now and then fight for your King and country, as every gentleman ought; and in a short time, I don't doubt, but I shall see you a Captain, or some great man,

rolling

rolling in wealth, which you have got out of the fpoils of your enemies."—" No, faid Jack, captain, that will never do—no tricks upon travellers—I know better what I have to expect if I enlift—I muft lie hard, live hard, expofe my life and limbs, every hour of the day, and be foundly cudgelled every now and then into the bargain."—" O'ons, cried the ferjeant, where did the young dog pick up all this? He is enough to make a whole company defert."—" No, faid Jack, they fhall never defert through me ; for though I know this, as I am at prefent out of employment, and have a great refpect for the character of a gentleman foldier, I will enlift directly in your regiment." " A brave fellow, indeed, faid the ferjeant; here, my boy, here is your money and your cockade," both which he directly prefented, for fear his recruit fhould change his mind; and thus in a moment little Jack became a foldier.

He had fcarcely time to feel himfelf eafy in his new accoutrements, before he was embarked for India in the character of a marine. This kind of life was entirely new to Jack ; however, his ufual activity and fpirit of obfervation did not defert him here, and he had not been embarked many weeks, before he was perfectly acquainted with all the duty of a failor, and in that refpect equal to moft on board. It happened that

that the fhip, in which he failed, touched at the Cormo Iflands, in order to take in wood

and water; thefe are fome little iflands near the coaft of Africa, inhabited by blacks. Jack often went on fhore with the officers, attending them on their fhooting parties to carry their powder and fhot, and the game they killed. All this country confifts of very lofty hills, covered with trees and fhrubs of various kinds, which never lofe their leaves, from the perpetual warmth of the climate. Through thefe it is frequently difficult to force a way, and the hills themfelves abound in precipices. It happened that one of the officers whom Jack was attending upon a fhooting party, took aim at fome great bird, and brought it down; but as it fell into fome deep valley, over fome rocks which it was impoffible to defcend, they defpaired of gaining their prey.

Jack,

Jack, immediately, with officious haste, set off and ran down the more level side of the hill, thinking to make a circuit and reach the valley into which the bird had fallen. He set off, therefore, but as he was totally ignorant of the country, he, in a short time, buried himself so deep in the wood, which grew continually thicker, that he knew not which way to proceed. He then thought it most prudent to return; but this he found as difficult to effect as the other. He therefore wandered about the woods with inconceivable difficulty all day, but could never find his company nor even reach the shore, or obtain the prospect of the sea. At length the night approached, and Jack, who perceived it to be impossible to do that in the dark, which he had not been able to effect in the light, lay down under a rock, and composed himself to rest, as well as he was able. The next day he rose with the light, and once more attempted to regain the shore: but unfortunately he had totally lost all idea of the direction he ought to pursue, and saw nothing around him but the dismal prospect of woods and hills and precipices, without a guide or path. Jack now began to be very hungry, but as he had a fowling piece with him, and powder and shot, he soon procured himself a dinner; and kindling a fire with some dry leaves and sticks, he roasted

his

his game upon the embers, and dined as com-

fortably as he could be expected to do, in fo forlorn a fituation. Finding himfelf much refrefhed, he purfued his journey, but with as little fuccefs as ever. On the third day, he indeed came in fight of the fea, but found that he was quite on a different fide of the ifland from that where he left the fhip, and that neither fhip nor boat was to be feen. Jack now loft all hopes of rejoining his comrades, for he knew the fhip was to fail at fartheft upon the third day, and would not wait for him. He, therefore, fat down very penfively upon a rock, and caft his eyes upon the vaft extent of ocean which was ftretched out before him. He found himfelf now abandoned upon a ftrange country, without a fingle friend, acquaintance, or even any one who fpoke the fame language. He

at

at first thought of seeking out the natives, and making known to them his deplorable state; but he began to fear the reception he might meet with among them. They might not be pleased, he thought, with his company, and might take the liberty of treating him as the white men generally treat the blacks when they get them into their poffeffion; that is, make him work hard with very little victuals, and knock him on the head if he attempted to run away. And therefore, says Jack, as he was meditating all alone, it may, perhaps, be better for me to stay quiet where I am. It is true, indeed, I shall not have much company to talk to, but then I shall have nobody to quarrel with me, or baa, or laugh at my poor daddy and mammy. Neither do I at present see how I shall get a livelihood, when my powder and shot are all expended; but however I shall hardly be starved, for I saw several kinds of fruit in the woods, and some roots which look very much like carrots. As to cloaths, when mine wear out, I shall not much want new ones; for the weather is charmingly warm; and therefore, all things confidered, I don't see why I should not be as happy here as in any other place.—When Jack had finished his speech, he set himself to find a lodging for the night. He had not examined far before he found a dry cavern in a rock, which

which he thought would prove a very comfortable
refidence; he therefore went to work with an
hatchet he had with him, and cut fome boughs
of trees, which he fpread upon the floor, and over
thofe a long filky kind of grafs, which he found in
plenty near the place, to make himfelf a bed. His
next care was, how to fecure himfelf in cafe of
any attack, for he did not know whether the ifland
contained any wild beafts or not. He therefore
cut down feveral branches of trees, and wove them
into a kind of wicker work, as he had feen the
men do hurdles when he lived with the farmer;
with this contrivance he found he could very fe-
curely barricade the entrance of his cave. And
now, as the evening was again approaching, he
begun to feel himfelf hungry, and feeking along
the fea-fhore, he found fome fhell-fifh, which
fupplied him with a plentiful meal. The next day
Jack arofe, a little melancholy indeed, but with a
refolution to ftruggle manfully with the difficulties of his fituation. He walked into the woods
and faw feveral kinds of fruit and berries, fome
of which he ventured to eat, as the birds had
pecked them, and found the tafte agreeable. He
alfo dug up feveral fpecies of roots, but feared to
tafte them left they fhould be poifonous. At
length, he felected one that very much refembled
a potatoe, and determined to roaft it in the embers,

bers, and taſte a very ſmall bit. It can hardly, thought Jack, do me much hurt, in ſo very ſmall a quantity; and if that agrees with me I will increaſe the doſe. The root was fortunately extremely wholeſome and nutritive, ſo that Jack was in a very ſhort time tolerably ſecure againſt the danger of wanting food. In this manner did Jack lead a kind of ſavage, but tolerably contented life, for ſeveral months; during which time he enjoyed perfect health, and was never diſcovered by any of the natives. He uſed ſeveral times a-day to viſit the ſhore, in hopes that ſome ſhip might paſs that way and deliver him from his ſolitary impriſonment. This, at length, happened, by the boat of an Engliſh ſhip, that was ſailing to India, happening to touch upon the coaſt; Jack inſtantly hailed the crew, and the

officer,

officer, upon hearing the story, agreed to receive him; the captain too, when he found that Jack was by no means a contemptible sailor, very willingly gave him his passage, and promised him a gratuity besides, if he behaved well.

Jack arrived in India without any accident, and relating his story, was permitted to serve in another regiment, as his own was no longer there. He soon distinguished himself by his courage and good behaviour on several occasions, and before long was advanced to the rank of a serjeant. In this capacity, he was ordered out upon an expedition into the remote parts of the country. The little army in which he served now marched on for several weeks, through a burning climate, and in want of all the necessaries of life. At length, they entered upon some extensive plains, which bordered upon the celebrated country of the Tartars. Jack was perfectly well acquainted with the history of this people, and their method of fighting. He knew them to be some of the best horsemen in the world; indefatigable in their attacks, though often repulsed returning to the charge, and not to be invaded with impunity; he, therefore, took the liberty of observing to some of the officers, that nothing could be more dangerous than their rashly engaging themselves in those extensive plains,

where

where they were every moment expofed to the attacks of cavalry, without any fuccefsful me-

thod of defence, or place of retreat, in cafe of any misfortune. Thefe remonftrances were not much attended to, and after a few hours farther march, they were alarmed by the approach of a confiderable body of Tartar horfemen. They, however, drew up with all the order they were able, and firing feveral fuccefsive vollies, endeavoured to keep the enemy at a diftance. But the Tartars had no defign of doing that with a confiderable lofs, which they were fure of doing with eafe and fafety. Inftead therefore of charging the Europeans, they contented themfelves with giving continual alarms, and menacing them on every fide, without expofing themfelves to any confiderable danger.

ger. The army now attempted to retreat, hoping that they should be able to arrive at the neighbouring mountains, where they would be safe from the incursions of the horse. But in this attempt they were equally disappointed; for another considerable body of enemies appeared on that side, and blocked their passage. The Europeans now found they were surrounded on all sides, and that resistance was vain. The commanding officer, therefore, judged it expedient to try what could be effected by negociation, and sent one of his officers, who understood something of the Tartar language, to treat with the general of the enemies. The Tartar chief received the Europeans with great civility, and after having gently reproached them with their ambition, in coming so far to invade a people who had never injured them, he consented upon very moderate conditions to their enlargement: but he insisted upon having their arms delivered up, except a very few which he permitted them to keep for defence in their return, and upon retaining a certain number of Europeans as hostages for the performance of the stipulated articles. Among those who were thus left with the Tartars Jack happened to be included, and while all the rest seemed inconsolable at being thus made prisoners by a barbarous nation, he alone, accustomed to all the vicissitudes of life, retained

ed his cheerfulnefs, and prepared to meet every reverfe of fortune with his ufual firmnefs.

The Tartars among whom Jack was now to refide, conftitute feveral different tribes or nations which inhabit an immenfe extent of country both in Europe and Afia. Their country is in general open and uncultivated, without cities or towns, fuch as we fee in England. The inhabitants themfelves are a bold and hardy race of men that live in fmall tents, and change their place of abode with the different feafons of the year. All their property confifts in herds of cattle, which they drive along with them from place to place; and upon whofe milk and flefh they fubfift. They are particularly fond of horfes, of which they have a fmall but excellent breed, hardy and indefatigable for the purpofes of war, and they excel in the management of them, beyond what is eafy to conceive. Immenfe herds of thefe animals wander loofe about the deferts, but marked with the particular mark of the perfon or tribe to which they belong. When they want any of thefe animals for ufe, a certain number of their young men jump upon their horfes with nothing but an halter to guide them, each carrying in his hand a pole with a noofe or cord at the end. When they come in fight of the herd, they purfue the horfe they wifh

to

to take at full fpeed, come up with him in fpite of his fwiftnefs, and never fail to throw the noofe about his neck as he runs. They are frequently known to jump upon young horfes that have paffed their whole life in the defert, and with only a girt around the animal's body to hold by, maintain their feat, in fpite of all his violent exertions, until they have wearied him out and reduced him into perfect obedience. Such was the nation with whom the lot of Jack was now to refide, nor was he long before he had an opportunity of fhewing his talents.

It happened that a favourite horfe of the chief was taken with a violent fever, and feemed to be in immediate danger of death. The Khan, for fo he is called among the Tartars, feeing his horfe grow hourly worfe, at length applied to the Europeans, to know if they could fuggeft any thing for his recovery. All the officers were profoundly ignorant of farriery; but when the application was made to Jack, he defired to fee the horfe, and with great gravity began to feel his pulfe, by paffing his hand within the animal's fore-leg; which gave the Tartars a very high idea of his ingenuity. Finding that the animal was in a high fever, he propofed to the Khan to let him blood, which he had learned to do very dexteroufly in England. He obtained permiffion to do as he pleafed,

pleafed, and having by great good luck a lancet with him, he let him blood very dexteroufly in the neck. After this operation he covered

him up, and gave him a warm potion made out of fuch ingredients as he could procure upon the fpot, and left him quiet. In a few hours the horfe began to mend, and, to the great joy of the Khan, perfectly recovered in a few days. This cure, fo opportunely performed, raifed the reputation of Jack fo high, that every body came to confult him about their horfes, and in a fhort time he was the univerfal farrier of the tribe. The Khan himfelf conceived fo great an affection for him, that he gave him an excellent horfe to rid upon and attend him in his hunting parties; and Jack, who excelled in the art or horfemanfhip,

mana-

managed him so well as to gain the esteem of the whole nation.

The Tartars, though they are excellent horsemen, have no idea of managing their horses, unless by violence; but Jack in a short time, by continual care and attention, made his horse so docile and obedient to every motion of his hand and leg, that the Tartars themselves would gaze upon him with admiration, and allow themselves to be outdone. Not contented with this, he procured some iron, and made his horse shoes in the European taste; this also was matter of astonishment to all the Tartars, who are accustomed to ride their horses unshod. He next observed that the Tartar saddles are all prodigiously large and cumbersome, raising the horseman up to a great distance from the back of his horse. Jack set himself to work, and was not long before

fore he had completed something like an English hunting saddle, on which he paraded before the Khan. All mankind seem to have a passion for novelty, and the Khan was so delighted with this effort of Jack's ingenuity, that, after paying him the highest compliments, he intimated a desire of having such a saddle for himself. Jack was the most obliging creature in the world, and spared no labour to serve his friends; he went to work again, and in a short time completed a saddle still more elegant for the Khan. These exertions gained him the favour and esteem both of the Khan and all the tribe; so that Jack was an universal favourite, and loaded with presents, while all the rest of the officers, who had never learned to make a saddle or an horse-shoe, were treated with contempt and indifference. Jack, indeed, behaved with the greatest generosity to his countrymen, and divided with them all the mutton and venison which were given him; but he could not help sometimes observing, that it was great pity they had not learned to make an horse-shoe instead of dancing and dressing hair.

And now an Ambassador arrived from the English settlements, with an account that all the conditions of the treaty had been performed, and demanding the restitution of the prisoners. The Tartar Chief was too much a man of honour to delay an instant, and they were all restored; but before

before they set out, Jack laboured with indefatigable zeal to finish a couple of saddles and a dozen horse-shoes, which he presented to the Khan, with many expressions of gratitude. The Khan was charmed with this proof of his affection, and in return made him a present of a couple of fine horses, and several valuable skins of beasts. Jack arrived without any accident at the English settlements, and selling his skins and horses, found himself in possession of a moderate sum of money. He now began to have a desire to return to England, and one of the officers, who had often been obliged to him during his captivity, procured him a discharge. He embarked, therefore, with all his property on board

a ship, which was returning home, and in a few months was safely landed at Plymouth.

But Jack was too active and too prudent to give

give himself up to idleness. After considering various schemes of business, he determined to take up his old trade of forging; and for that purpose made a journey into the North, and found his old master alive, and as active as ever. His master, who had always entertained an esteem for Jack, welcomed him with great affection, and being in want of a foreman, he engaged him at a very handsome price for that place. Jack was now indefatigable in the execution of his new office; inflexibly honest where the interests of his master were concerned, and at the same time humane and obliging to the men who were under him, he gained the affection of all about him. In a few years, his master was so thoroughly convinced of his merit, that growing old himself, he took Jack into partnership, and committed the management of the whole business to his care. He continued to exert the same qualities now which he had done before, by which means he improved the business so much, as to gain a considerable fortune, and become one of the most respectable manufacturers in the country.—But, with all this prosperity, he never discovered the least pride or haughtiness; on the contrary, he employed part of his fortune to purchase the moor where he formerly lived, and built himself a small, but convenient house, upon the very spot where his daddy's dy's hut had formerly stood. Hither he would sometimes retire from business, and cultivate his garden with his own hands, for he hated idleness.

To all his poor neighbours he was kind and liberal, relieving them in their distress, and often entertaining them at his house, where he used to dine with them, with the greatest affability, and frequently relate his own story, in order to prove that it is of very little consequence how a man comes into the world, provided he behaves well, and discharges his duty when he is in it.

A SKETCH OF UNIVERSAL HISTORY.

ADVERTISEMENT.

THE following Sketch of Universal History was written by a gentleman for the use of two young ladies, and not intended for publication; but as it was designed to supply what he thought was wanting to give the minds of children some idea of general history, and as it perfectly answered the purpose for which he composed it, he has been induced to publish it, that others might reap the same advantage which those have for whose use it was particularly composed.

There are, it is true, many abridgments of Sacred, Greek, Roman, and English History; but some short sketch of General History seems wanting, that the learner may be enabled to see how the separate parts are connected with each other. This deficiency is here attempted to be supplied; and as young minds are too volatile to be long fixed, it is drawn on as small a scale as possible: on the same account it was thought proper not to load it with chronological dates, but to throw it into a concise and simple narrative, that the connection of the successive events with each other might be readily acquired, and easily retained when acquired.

The

The author has carefully avoided the giving a greater space to those circumstances which are nearest the present time; for though in larger histories this must necessarily happen, from the increasing quantity of materials, yet it is a fault in a work of this sort, since it tends to impress on the ductile imagination of youth wrong ideas of chronology, which are not easily eradicated, as the mind will be apt to connect the length of the æra with the number of the pages it occupies.

The author of these sheets is free to confess, that his own imagination, even in riper years, was so much biassed by this early prejudice, that it cost some pains to correct it; and he will venture to say, that many persons of no inconsiderable historical knowledge will find the time bestowed on a careful perusal of this Sketch, accompanied with an inspection of Doctor Priestley's Historical and Biographical Charts, by no means thrown away.

A SKETCH, &c.

THE earliest information we have of the actions of mankind is from the Holy Scriptures. We have there an account of the creation of the world, the destruction of it by the Flood, the renewal of mankind by the family of Noah,

Noah, who were preserved in the Ark, and their increase and difperfion over the whole face of the earth. The Scriptures then proceed principally with the hiftory of the defcendants of Abraham, whofe great grandfon, Jofeph, fettling in Egypt with his eleven brothers, they became, with their progeny, flaves to that powerful people. But increafing in procefs of time, they migrated from thence, and fettled in Paleftine, after many wars, expelling the old inhabitants, who are called, in our tranflation of the Bible, Philiftines. The defcendants of Abraham ftiled themfelves Ifraelites, or children of Ifrael, from Jacob, the father of Jofeph, who was alfo named Ifrael. They divided the country among their twelve tribes, diftinguifhed by the names of the twelve fons of Jacob, from whom they were feverally defcended. At firft, they were governed by magiftrates, called Judges; and afterwards by Kings. In the reign of Rehoboam, their fourth King, fon to Solomon, and grandfon to David, ten of the tribes revolted, under a leader named Jeroboam, leaving two tribes only, viz. Juda and Benjamin, under Rehoboam, whofe defcendants were called Kings of Juda, from whence the name of Jews was derived; and the fucceffors of Jeroboam were called Kings of Ifrael.

Several powerful nations arofe in their neighbourhood, which all became in time fubject to the

the empire of Affyria. To fuch a formidable enemy the offspring of Abraham were an eafy conqueft: the ten tribes of Ifrael were carried into captivity, and their name no more heard of among the nations: the chief perfons among the Jews were alfo carried to Babylon, the capital of Affyria; but the people were permitted to remain at home under the dominion of their conquerors.

Soon after this a new power arofe. The King of Affyria turned his arms againft the Medes and Perfians. Cambyfes, King of Perfia, had married Mandane, daughter of Aftyages, King of Media. The firft attack of the Affyrians was againft Media. The Perfians fent Cyrus, fon of Cambyfes and Mandane, at the head of an army, to the affiftance of his uncle Cyaxares, who was then King. The invader was repelled, invaded in his turn, the King of Affyria killed at the taking of Babylon, and the whole empire reduced under the dominion of the Medes and Perfians, over both of whom Cyrus reigned, by marrying the only daughter of his uncle Cyaxares. Thus was the Perfian empire founded.

The Perfian empire extended over all the known parts of Afia: and the ambition of Darius, a fucceffor, though not a defcendant of Cyrus, induced him to attempt the conqueft of part of of Europe; but here he met with a severe repulse from the Grecian republics.

This small people, who inhabited a country of narrow extent, were not only able, by their courage and military skill, to check this powerful invader, but they had made such a proficiency in wisdom and arts, that we may now say, every attainment modern Europe has made in both, is principally, if not solely derived from them. The origin of this singular people is very uncertain. The first time they made any conspicuous figure in the annals of mankind, was in the Trojan war, which has been rendered immortal by the poems of Homer. At that time they were divided into small kingdoms, under limited monarchs; all of which, before the Persian invasion, were formed into republics.

The Persian King Darius despised such feeble antagonists; but both he and his son Xerxes soon learned, by fatal experience, the advantage of valour and discipline over timid multitudes. After the loss of immense armies, the Kings of Persia contented themselves with fomenting the differences which began to arise among the Grecian republics, in which Athens and Sparta took the lead; and remaining anxious spectators of the bloody wars which they made with each other, when freed from the apprehensions of a foreign enemy.

While

While Greece was thus wasting her strength in wars at home, great jealousy was still entertained lest the common enemy (for so the King of Persia was esteemed) should take advantage of her weakness to accomplish his ambitious designs, when a storm unexpectedly burst on them from another quarter.

There was a country to the north of Greece, called Macedonia, which, though in many respects congenial with it, was looked on as barbarous (for the Greeks called all nations but themselves Barbarians). Macedonia was governed by an absolute King. Philip, Prince of Macedonia, happening, on some occasion, to be an hostage among the Greeks, had the advantage, at the same time, of learning their art of war, and seeing their internal dissentions. Profiting by this knowledge, when he succeeded to the throne of Macedonia, he so contrived to embroil the affairs of Greece by corruption and intrigue; and by taking part sometimes with one party, and sometimes with another, so to weaken the whole, that, having bribed the Chiefs of some of the republics to his interest, and totally defeated the Athenians and their allies at the battle of Chæronea, he rendered Greece entirely dependent on himself.

Knowing, however, the difficulty of keeping such a people in peaceable subjection, he planned the popular scheme of an invasion of Persia; assembling for this purpose the whole force of Greece, and causing himself to be acknowledged Chief of the confederacy. In the midst of this undertaking he was assassinated, and was succeeded in his power by his son, distinguished by the appellation of Alexander the Great.

Alexander, immediately putting himself at the head of this formidable army, conquered the Persian empire, with all its dependencies, and, penetrating to the banks of the Ganges, subdued even part of that country so well known to us by the name of the East-Indies. But this immense empire was of short duration; for, on his return, he died at Babylon, as some say, by poison, as others by excessive drinking, leaving his vast dominions to be divided among his Generals. Asia, Egypt, and Greece, exhibited a continual scene of war and desolation, especially Greece, where there were perpetual struggles between the successors of Alexander for dominion and the republics for liberty, till the whole was reduced to subjection by the power of Rome.

Rome, which makes so conspicuous a figure in the history of mankind, arose from being a small state to the utmost extent of territory and power. At first it was governed by Kings, who were expelled for their tyranny, and two annual magistrates chosen in their place; these, with

the

the senate and assemblies of the people, formed the government, not unlike our King, Lords, and Commons. The Romans soon engaged in wars with the other states of Italy, all of which they finally conquered; increasing by those means not only their strength but their military knowledge; and as many of the Italian states were Greek colonies, they had all the advantage of the Grecian art of war, improved by their own experience. Being masters of Italy, they turned their arms against Sicily, which engaged them in a war with Carthage, a powerful state on the north of Africa, who had colonies in that island. This war was prosecuted with various success, till the perseverance and courage of the Romans prevailed, and Carthage was totally subdued.

To return to the affairs of Greece: Rome made the assisting the Greek republics a pretence for interfering in their disputes, and finally reduced both the oppressors and the oppressed to an entire dependence on herself.

The armies of Rome now became invincible. Not only Asia, Egypt, Greece, and the northern parts of Africa, were subdued, but she extended her conquests to Spain, Gaul, and Britain.

Yet, amid these splendid scenes of victory abroad, Rome was torn to pieces by factions at home. At first the struggles were between the senate and the people, till particular persons
obtaining

obtaining power by holding long commands abroad, the names of the popular, or noble party were only used as skreens to the ambition of individuals. The last great contest was between Julius Cæsar and Pompey; the first of whom had commanded in the northern, and the other in the eastern provinces. The decisive battle of Pharsalia, and the subsequent death of Pompey, gave the whole Roman empire into the hands of Cæsar. The spirit of liberty, however, made one dying effort. Cæsar was stabbed in the senate house, and an army raised in defence of public freedom. But after a short war, the veteran troops of Cæsar, under command of Octavius, his nephew and adopted heir, Marcus Antonius, his friend, and Lepidus, one of his generals, defeated the army of the republic, and the three leaders divided the empire among them.

Lepidus, being a weak man, was soon deposed; and M. Antonius, devoted to his pleasures, shut himself up in Egypt with Cleopatra, the queen of that country. Octavius Cæsar, taking advantage of his indolence, encroached on his provinces, and a war ensuing, Antonius was totally defeated at the naval battle of Actium, soon after which he killed himself, and Octavius remained sole master of the Roman empire, with the title of Emperor, and the name

of

of Auguſtus Cæſar; and Rome, with its vaſt territories, from this period became ſubject to the dominion of an arbitrary monarch.

Our Saviour was born during the reign of Auguſtus, and ſuffered crucifixion under Tiberius, his immediate ſucceſſor.

From this time the whole civilized world being under one maſter, hiſtory for a long period has little elſe to record than the characters of the Roman Emperors; and mankind were happy or miſerable as their governors were mild or cruel. Perhaps the ſtate of the human race was never more enviable than when ſuch characters as Titus, Trajan, or the Antonines, were maſters of the world. While under the government of ſuch monſters, as Caligula, Nero, and Domitian, who ſeemed to delight only in cruelty, mankind were in the moſt miſerable ſituation, unable either to reſiſt the power of the tyrant, or eſcape from his dominions, as there was no country out of the limits of the Roman empire that was not inhabited by the moſt ſavage barbarians. It may not be amiſs here to mention, that, under the reign of Titus, tenth Emperor from Auguſtus, the city of Jeruſalem, after repeated rebellions, was finally deſtroyed by the Romans, and the Jews diſperſed, as they remain at this day: a ſingular inſtance of a people, who having loſt their country, ſtill maintain, though
ſcattered

scattered over the face of the earth, their religion, their language, and their laws, the same as they were at a period far beyond any antiquity to which the annals of any the most ancient nation extend.

Though the barbarous tribes that bordered on the Roman empire were continually infesting the frontiers with hostilities, and gradually encroaching on its provinces, yet it suffered no great diminution of territory till after the time of Constantine, who was the forty-first Emperor in succession from Augustus, and lived upwards of three hundred years after him.

During that period Christianity had been gradually, though privately, extending itself. The professors of it had been cruelly persecuted by some of the Emperors, and tolerated by others; but Constantine was the first Emperor who openly professed to be a Christian, and from his time Christianity became the established religion of the empire.

Constantine, from an absurd vanity, removed the imperial seat from Rome to a city of his own building, between the Mediterranean and Euxine Seas, which he called Constantinopolis, or the city of Constantine; and on his death he divided the empire between his sons. From this time the Roman empire consisted of two parts; the one, whose seat continued at Rome, was called

called the Western Empire; the other, whose capital was Constantinople, was called the Eastern, and sometimes the Grecian Empire.

The empire, being thus divided, grew consequently weaker, and the inroads of the barbarous nations more formidable. The Goths and Vandals attacked the Western Empire. The Franks, a brave, though uncivilized people, possessed themselves of Gaul, from whom it received the name of France. The Britons, on being abandoned by Rome to the inroads of the savage tribes in the north of the island, called in the Saxons to their assistance, who soon made themselves masters of the whole, except the mountains of Wales and Scotland, which afforded an asylum to the ancient inhabitants. And Rome, itself, under Augustulus, the last of its Emperors, was taken by Odoacer, King of the Heruli.

The Eastern empire was attacked by the Saracens, a fierce people, who had embraced the religion of Mahomet, an impostor, and founder of a new sect, whose doctrine soon spread, and still retains its influence, in the East. This warlike race conquered Arabia, Syria, Egypt, and the northern coasts of Africa; but they were, in their turn, expelled by the Turks, a nation of Scythian origin, who adopted the religion and manners of the vanquished. The provinces of
the

the Eaſtern empire gradually mouldered away, till it was at laſt confined to the walls of Conſtantinople. A final period was put to the Roman empire ſo late as the year of our Lord 1453, when Conſtantinople was taken by Mahomet, Sultan of the Turks, of whoſe dominion it has ever ſince remained the capital. This happened under Conſtantine X. (the hundred and fourteenth Emperor in ſucceſſion from Auguſtus), who was killed in the aſſault, 2200 years from the foundation of Rome, and during the reign of Henry VI. of England.

This was the real end of the Roman empire; but previous to this, ſo early as the year of our Lord 800, there was a pretended revival of it in the perſon of Charlemagne, or Charles the Great.

The barbarous tribes who overturned the Roman empire, having very obſcure notions of any religion, eaſily adopted that of the people they conquered; and as the Saracens, and after them the Turks, who ravaged the Eaſt, embraced the errors of Mahomet, which they found eſtabliſhed in Arabia, ſo the northern barbarians who conquered Gaul, Germany, and Italy, were eaſily converted to the faith of Chriſt: and the Biſhop of Rome, who aſſumed the title of Pope, and Patriarch of the Roman church, ſoon obtained the

the fame influence over the Heruli, and the Lombards, who fucceeded them, as he had over the Romans under their Chriftian Emperors. But Defiderius, the Lombard King of Italy, oppofing the ambition of Pope Stephen III. the Pope called Charlemagne, King of France, to his aid, who dethroned Defiderius and conquered Italy: as a reward for which, the Pope crowned him Emperor at Rome; and Charlemagne becoming afterwards mafter of Germany, and dividing his dominions between his fons, that to whom Germany fell retained the title of Roman Emperor, which his fucceffors ftill continue to affume: and the head of a limited elective monarchy, who refides at Vienna, now calls himfelf Emperor of the Romans, and takes the names of Cæfar and Auguftus.

About the fame time that Charlemagne made thefe conquefts on the continent of Europe, Egbert united the feven provinces into which the Saxons had divided all the fouthern part of this ifland (except Wales) into one kingdom by the name of England.

Thefe barbarians were no fooner fettled in their conquefts, and in fome degree civilized, than a frefh inundation poured in from the north, under the name of Danes and Normans, and, committing the fame ravages on the new poffeffors which they had committed on the old inhabitants,

inhabitants, at last fixed themselves, part in Germany, part in England, and part in that province of France which yet retains the name of Normandy; and, as their predecessors had done, soon assumed the religion and manners of the vanquished.

As these northern nations settled over all the western parts of Europe, which were divided by them into many states, so the same form of government, derived from the same origin, was established in them all. The leader of each army of invaders was considered as King, and in some measure as proprietor, of the conquered territory. But as it was necessary to have an army ready at all times to repel new invaders, and guard against the encroachment of neighbours, the King, or General, parcelled out his land among the superior officers, who, by way of acknowledgment, were bound to furnish him with a proportionable assistance of men and arms in time of war, and to attend his councils in time of peace. And these leaders, to enable themselves to command the requisite number of troops which they were to furnish, allotted part of their lands again to the inferior officers and soldiers, on condition that they should attend them to the wars when summoned by the King or the Lord Paramount. And this, which is called the feudal system, is the origin of that li-
mitted

mitted monarchy, which, till within thefe two centuries, was eftablifhed throughout the greateft part of Europe, and which this ifland has been fo happy as to preferve.

Civilization has as yet made but a fmall progrefs: the writings of the ancient Greeks and Romans, which are now the models of every thing great and elegant, were confined to the hands of a bigotted clergy; and war was the fole delight of princes and nobles too ignorant even to write their names.

This warlike fpirit, however, was attended by fome good confequences: for the Saracens, who had overrun the eaftern parts of Europe, began to turn their arms againft the fouthern parts of weftern Europe; they threatened Italy, invaded the fouthern part of France, their African colonies had made themfelves mafters of the beft part of Spain, and nothing lefs than the warlike turn of its inhabitants could have prevented all Europe from becoming a prey to thefe fierce barbarians, and the confequent rudenefs and defpotifm which ever have attended the religion of Mahomet wherever it prevails.

The Chriftian Doctrine, corrupted as it was by the Church of Rome, had yet a tendency to polifh and foften the manners of its profeffors; and even the power of the Pope, whofe fupre-

macy

macy was acknowledged by so many independent and turbulent princes, though often used for the purposes of superstition, was sometimes also instrumental in stopping the progress, or mitigating the horrors of war.

A new spirit of enterprize now took place in Europe. As the zeal for Christianity increased, the warlike princes and nobles who professed it, beheld with indignation the scene of all the miracles, recorded both in the Old and New Testament, in the hands of infidels. The Pope encouraged this religious fervour; and vast armies were poured forth to rescue these consecrated seats from the Mahometans. But, after deluging the plains of Palestine with Christian blood, and making a conquest of Jerusalem, which could not be retained, the votaries of Mahomet remained, and still remain, possessors of that country which is commonly called the Holy Land.

Some advantage, however, was derived from these enterprizes. Part of the immense armies that passed from Europe to Asia, took their route by Constantinople; and though, to their shame it must be owned, that while their end was to rescue part of Asia from the power of infidels, they themselves committed devastation in the dominions of the only Christian Prince in the east of Europe, yet they were struck with
the

the magnificence of the court of Conftantinople, where fome relics of the fplendour of the Roman Empire were ftill preferved. This introduced a tafte for the arts among the Princes of weftern Europe; and on the Turks putting an end to the eaftern empire by the capture of Conftantinople, the learned men of that city migrated into France, Italy, Germany and Britain, and introduced there a knowledge of Grecian literature.

Happily for the revival of learning, Leo X. who was then Pope, was as defirous of extending literature as fome of his predeceffors had been of fpreading ignorance: he therefore entertained the Grecian exiles, and encouraged letters among the clergy. At this time Europe was in a more pacific ftate: England breathed after the long wars between York and Lancafter: France, from being divided among a number of independent nobles, each able to awe the titular King, became one powerful monarchy: the Moors were driven out of Spain, and that whole country, which had formed many feparate kingdoms, was united by the marriage of Ferdinand of Caftile and Ifabella of Arragon: Germany was one large republic of Princes, of whom the Emperor was the head; and Italy was divided into many fmall ftates, the chief of which

which were the kingdom of Naples, and the commonwealth of Venice.

The Pope now found his authority ſhaken. As literature advanced, a ſpirit of inquiry took place, and the monſtrous errors grafted by the church of Rome on the pure religion of Chriſt began to be perceived. Luther and Calvin pub-liſhed their opinions on this ſubject, and had many followers, who, from proteſting againſt the errors of the church of Rome, obtained the name of Proteſtants; and their opinions prevail-ed in England, the northern countries, and part of Germany and Switzerland.

About this time the art of navigation being greatly improved, a large continent was diſ-covered in the weſt, called America. Many colonies were ſoon formed there by the Engliſh, French and Spaniards, which have occaſioned frequent wars among thoſe nations. From this period, as commerce has increaſed, mankind have become more civilized. Religion and po-litics for a time filled both England and France with inteſtine commotions. Charles I. of Eng-land was brought to the ſcaffold by his ſubjects, and Henry IV. of France was ſtabbed by an enthuſiaſt. But at length theſe ſtorms have ſub-ſided. By the arts of Lewis XIV. France is brought to be an abſolute monarchy, without any

any legal restraint, indeed, on the power of the crown; but as that crown derives all its stability from a gallant noblesse, jealous to a degree of their honour, that honour must be respected, and is a sufficient barrier against any wanton exertion of despotism. The spirit of the people of England has obtained them a form of government which is the envy of the world.

The history of these nations, eternal rivals in glory and interest, for the two last centuries, is in fact the history of the world. During that period, there has been no war of any consequence between European powers in any part of the world in which they have not acted a principal part; and a war between them extends its influence from the shores of America to the banks of the Ganges. They have been constantly ready to attack each other on the most trivial occasions, and even their treaties of peace have seemed rather cessations of hostilities for the purpose of renewing them with greater vigour, than any permanent reconciliation. May the present commercial intercourse lead to better hopes, and may the only contest for the future be, who shall excel most in the arts of peace and the pursuits of literature!

EPISTLE TO A FRIEND,

ON HIS RETURN FROM THE ARMY.

AT length, war's bloody banners furl'd,
Peace spreads her influence o'er the world;
Great George his laurel crown resigns,
And round his brow the olive twines;
You from the martial field retreat,
To seek your old paternal seat,
And, after five years absence, come
Loaded with debts and glory home.
Of tender parents favorite son,
Behold their happiness begun:
No more the Gazette's glorious tale
Now makes their anxious features pale,
Lest on the verdant laurel's stem
The cypress dark should grow for them.
Joyful they hail the morning ray,
And hope expectant gilds the day;
For sure, they cry, ere close of light,
Our absent son will bless our sight.
Till eve they watch with aching eyes,
And the next morn new hopes supplies.
And now the wish'd-for hour draws near,
That drowns in transport every fear;
Blest comfort of their waning lives,
Their son, their much lov'd son, arrives!—
On either side your bosoms glow,
And mutual tears of rapture flow;
I see, I see your generous breast
With filial love and joy possess'd:

I feel,

RETURN FROM THE ARMY.

I feel, my friend! that joy impart
Fire to my sympathizing heart,
And bid my artless pen portray
The scenes that fancy's dreams display.
 While yet still night, in sable robe,
Broods o'er our quarter of the globe;
While slumber wraps each labouring breast,
And care herself is sooth'd to rest,
Alone impatient of delay,
Your thoughts anticipate the day:
You rouse at once from Morpheus' reign
The landlord and his menial train;
The drowsy ostler cries in vain,
" 'Tis dark, you cannot see your hand:
Booted and spurr'd you ready stand,
And mounting swift your eager steed,
Fearless through night and cold proceed.
 Soon as Aurora's ruddy ray
Beams forth to chear you on your way,
I see you sweep, with loosen'd rein,
O'er hill and dale, thro' wood and plain;
Now gallop down the steep, and now,
Climbing the mountain's loftiest brow,
Bend o'er the landscape wide your eye,
Anxious your sire's abode to spy:
The fleeting spot eludes your view,
And seems to fly as you pursue.—
Faint on the horizon's farthest mound,
What hill is that with pine trees crown'd?
The well-known landmark strikes your sight;
Your bosom swells with fond delight;

Fancy

Fancy vain hope no longer yields:
" Ye much-lov'd fhades! ye blooming fields!
" My eager fteps," you cry, " once more"
" Your green receffes fhall explore."
And now, as with redoubled fpeed
Forward you urge your bounding fteed,
You fee the well-known fpire arife,
And point its fummit to the fkies;
And now, each envious barrier paft,
With heart-felt blifs you view at laft
The turrets of the Gothic dome,
Your parents' venerable home.
Here memory's fond powers difpenfe
Their influence o'er each raptur'd fenfe.
'Twas here, to pay a mother's care,
You firft imbib'd the vital air ;
Here each paternal art exprefs'd,
To foothe and charm your infant breaft,
Taught you in opening youth to prove
The blifs fincere of filial love.
Think how your parents' bofoms burn
To welcome your long-wifh'd return;
Torn from their arms by glory's power,
How have they told each tedious hour!
Already to your eyes appear
The faultering voice, the joyful tear.

 Befide the road the peafants throng
To fee you fwiftly pafs along;
And bowing as you gallop by,
" 'Tis the young Captain, fure," they cry:
On you their greetings are all loft,
Forward with eager zeal you poft;

       To-morrow

To-morrow you'll return each bow,
But warmer duties call you now.
Arriv'd, at length, you touch once more
Your father's hospitable door.
The cheerful family surround
The hearth with crackling faggots crown'd;
Some friends partake the genial ray,
Nor is the parish priest away.
Of taxes, hay, and war, they chat,
Of news and weather, this and that;
Of the young soldier too they spoke,
When a loud knock the converse broke.
Astonish'd by a sound so loud,
Around the window quick they crowd.
When screams of joy their bliss declare,
" 'Tis he, 'tis Belville come, I swear!"
Your parents, sisters, round you throng,
And transport loosens every tongue:
Your sire exclaims, " Five years are past
" Since I beheld my Belville last:
" Your country call'd you to the field,
" And I no more her sword could wield;
" Well hast thou fill'd thy father's place,
" Brave scyon of a warlike race:
" Nor shall my arms your steps detain,
" If fame and Britain call again."
O'er the brave vet'ran's furrow'd cheek
The beams of martial ardor break;
And from the eye where courage glows,
The tear of fond affection flows.
With silent joy your mother stands,
And grasps with trembling bliss your hands:

Her present hopes, her future fears,
Call forth alternate smiles and tears;
And in her face those thoughts are shewn;
Which anxious mothers feel alone.
Your sisters, too, the transport share,
And, with soft friendship's mildest air,
Demand if still your bosom prove
The fondness of fraternal love.
" How tedious pass'd," they cry, " the day,
" When our lov'd brother was away:
" You promis'd you would often write;
" But the old proverb—Out of sight"—
   Now ardent friendship's kindling joy,
And filial love, your thoughts employ;
And all the feelings of your breast
Are on your blooming cheek express'd:
A thousand questions, fondly made,
By fond caresses are delay'd;
Transport forbids your words to flow,
Nor can you answer yes, or no.
And see the ancient dame appears,
The fosterer of your infant years:
" Lord bless me! how young master's grown!
" I scarce should have the Captain known
" Elsewhere, unless I had been told:
" How well he looks in red and gold!
" Thank Heaven he has neither maim or wound,
" But comes again quite safe and found:
" For war's at best a dangerous choice;
" Good Sirs! how Madam must rejoice!"—
   What social bliss! what charming ties!
From parents, country, friends, arise.

May

May they who scorn their rights to know,
Ne'er feel the transports they bestow!
And far from me and those I love,
That stubborn breast, kind Heaven, remove,
Who meets unmov'd a mother's face,
Who tearless feels a friend's embrace;
Nor smiles to see those scenes rever'd,
Which infant pastimes have endear'd.

THE LITTLE QUEEN.

THERE reigned once upon a time, in a distant island, a good Prince, who was passionately beloved by all his subjects. It could not happen otherwise, for he was their common father. He provided for all their reasonable wants, he rewarded those who deserved well of their country, and he let none of the wicked, nor even of the idle, escape without punishment. This amiable Monarch had but one cause of anxiety; Myra, his only child, by no means requited the attention which had been given to her education. At twelve years of age she was shamefully ignorant. Her thoughtlessness made her forget every lesson which she had been taught, and her presumption kept pace with her want of knowledge; of consequence, as she thought herself perfectly accomplished, she despised all instruction. One day she was indulging her abfurd vanity by hinting, that were fhe to govern the ifland, things would be better managed than they were now. The King, having been informed of his daughter's fentiments, fent for her immediately. On her coming, he told her, without the leaft difcompofure, "That as "fhe was deftined to reign, one day or other, "over his kingdoms, he fhould wifh to know "how far her talents were proper for fo impor- "tant a charge. We may, if you pleafe," added this good Prince, "make the experiment "without any delay. Carelefs as you always were "about the leffons which have been given you "in geography, you cannot but know that *The* "*Fortunate Ifland* makes a part of my domi- "nions; it is a fmall, but well inhabited dif- "trict; its people are active, induftrious, good "tempered, and thoroughly attached to their "Sovereigns. Go, child! reign over them, I "fhall order a yacht to be inftantly fitted up to "convey you to your capital." Then making a moft profound reverence to the little Sovereign, "Adieu, madam," faid he, with difficulty concealing a fmile.

Myra, for fome time, thought that the King meant only to divert himfelf, but foon found her miftake, and that every thing was preparing for her voyage. She was even permitted to form a court to her own mind, and accordingly

fhe

she picked out a dozen of her playfellows to accompany her. "These young people," said she to her father, "are so very rational and sedate, "that there can be no need of their being at-"tended by governesses or tutors." The King, however, thought otherwise, and ordered the teachers to embark with their pupils. The young Sovereign, on her part, took care there should be abundance of musicians for her balls, and that a company of players should be provided for the amusement of herself and her court. On the morn of her departure, she took an affectionate leave of her father, but the few tears which she shed were soon dried up by the consideration of her being going to a place where she should do "just what she pleased." "The "only advice that I shall give you," said the King at parting, "is, that you would follow the "advice of Aristus (the Governor of the island "over which you are to reign) in every thing of "importance. He is a man for whom I have a "high esteem, and with reason, as he is discreet, "honest, and humane. I could wish that you "would make him your first Minister; I mean, "that you should consult him in every thing, and "entrust him with the execution of all your or-"ders."

This direction no way suited the taste of our young Queen, who wished to have given that important charge to one of her favourites, Philintus, listus, a tall, genteel lad, not, indeed, many years older than herself, but one who, to tolerable skill in dancing and singing, added the very agreeable talent of elegant flattery. He was himself as averse to study, and of consequence as ignorant as his royal mistress; but he had knowledge enough of his own interest to excite him never to omit assuring her that every one looked on her as a model of a perfect Princess, although he was conscious that, out of her hearing, she was universally blamed for being so totally unlike her excellent father, and for spending her whole time in trifling amusements.

As soon as the little Sovereign reached her island, she beheld with pleasure troops of shepherds and shepherdesses, in elegant fancy dresses of rose colour and white, who sung carols in praise of their new Queen, strewed sweet-scented flowers in her path, and presented her with odoriferous nosegays. Myra, charmed with this specimen of her subjects gallantry, ordered money to be distributed amongst them; and, under the conduct of Aristus, repaired to a lovely, though small palace, fitted up for her reception. Fatigued with the voyage, the Queen and her young court made haste to their repose; but her Majesty forgot not to order, for the next day, a comedy to be acted, followed by a ball and a splendid entertainment. On the next morn,
Myra

Myra and her court amused themselves by walking into the capital town, which lay not far from the palace. "Observe," said Aristus to his Sovereign, "the air of content which reigns in every "face we meet." "That," said Philintus, "we "should attribute to the presence of our lovely "Queen."—"Without doubt," replied Aristus, "they are sensible of that honour; but I ought "to inform you, that their gaiety is chiefly ow- "ing to their being conscious of the excellent "government under which they live, and of the "wisdom of those laws by which their King, "whom they look upon as their father, governs "the country."—"Let us now," said Myra, "extend our walks into the country." They did so. An orchard, in full bloom, now tempted her to take a nearer view of its beauty."— "What," said she to Aristus, "occasions the "buzzing sounds which I hear?"—"The bees," replied he; "a useful tribe of your Majesty's "subjects." At that instant, most unfortunately one of these animals, not perfectly acquainted with the respect due to royalty, and disgusted at the Queen's approaching too near to his hive, settled on her hand, and made her feel his sting! —"Shocking creatures, these bees!" exclaimed Myra; "one of them has half killed me!"— "The presumptuous, ungrateful wretches ought," said Philintus, "to be utterly extirpated."—

"You

"You are right," said the Queen; "I will have them destroyed, not on my own account, but to preserve my poor people from receiving such cruel wounds, when they are pursuing their occupations in the country." "Permit me," said Aristus, "to observe, that these accidents happen but very seldom, and that the pain which the bees occasion by their stings, is trifling, when compared with the vast advantage which accrues from their labours; your subjects, madam, will suffer severely indeed, if they are deprived of that useful creature."—Here he was interrupted by Philintus, who, bursting with laughter, cried out, "A pretty tale you tell us, Aristus! why, sure you take us all for children! Suffer indeed! what! because that nasty insect is kept from stinging them! Make us believe *that* if you can."—"I will have every bee in my kingdom put to death," said the young Queen, with an air of dignity.—"Possibly," said Aristus, "your Majesty may see cause hereafter to repent of this hasty command."—"Nevertheless," repeated Myra, "it *shall* be executed." Aristus retired with a sigh, and Philintus loudly applauded the mingled humanity and firmness of his infant Sovereign. That evening the Queen entertained herself at the play, and afterwards was present at a ball, which,

THE LITTLE QUEEN. 85

which, with a magnificent supper, lasted until two in the morning.

Unluckily, among the ladies of the bedchamber were two, who, not having reached their eleventh year, had been used to eat little or no suppers, to take moderate exercise, and to go to bed early. But the royal banquet had been so tempting, the ball so charming, and the whole so perfectly new to them, that they had despised the admonitions of their governesses, who had very naturally remonstrated against their launching at once into this new system. In consequence, they were both extremely ill the next morning. The physician attended, and ordered proper medicines, which they refused to take. "They were permitted by the Queen," they said, "to do what they liked best, and they "hated nasty physic." Their complaints, however, increased; they could neither eat, drink, or sleep, and one of the two felt the attack of a fever. On this the governesses were obliged to have recourse to the royal authority, and the Queen having commanded the young ladies to submit to discipline, they took what was ordered, and all went right again.

One day that the young Queen was walking in the garden of her palace, she was disgusted at the devastation which had been made by caterpillars on the leaves of the trees. "What
"vile

"vile creatures are these?" said she to Philintus: "Did you ever see such a piece of work as they have made here?"—"I think," replied the courtier, "that it would be a good deed to root them out of the island, and to proclaim rewards for those who would undertake to destroy them."—"What say you to that, Aristus," said Myra, "can my subjects exist without caterpillars?"—"Your Majesty," replied Aristus, "has not forgot the bees, I find, but here the case is widely different. The caterpillars which have stripped those trees do much mischief, and are of no one use to society."—"I am heartily glad," said the Queen, "that we coincide in opinion, for I am determined to have all the caterpillars in my dominions destroyed; I hate them, nasty creatures!"—"Your Majesty," said Aristus, "certainly means to except from this general massacre that kind of caterpillar which produces the silk worm."—"Do but hear him," said Philintus, in the Queen's ear, "that fellow makes a point of contradicting your Majesty in every thing."—"Let every caterpillar in my realm be put to death," exclaimed the piqued Sovereign.

"I am tired to death," said Myra one day, "of this eternal verdure. These walks of turf, and these clumps of laurel, though I like them well enough on the whole, yet being repeated

"peated fo often, they fatigue my eyes;—
" green, and green, and nothing but green—
" Why can I not have a rofe-colour bower?"
Philintus now turned all his thoughts towards the accomplifhment of his Sovereign's rational wifh. He had obferved in a diftant part of the garden an arbour where a honeyfuckle overfpread the green frame work. He ordered the leaves to be ftripped off, the wood to be painted rofe colour, and he covered the whole with artificial rofes hanging by crimfon ribbands. The Queen was enchanted with this gaudy retreat, and as foon as fhe faw it, ordered her dinner to be fet out upon that very fpot. The fun fhone out with great power, and fcarce had the company fate ten minutes at their meal, before fome complained of aching heads, fome of dazzled eyes; all loft their appetites, and the whole was a confufion of heat and glare. Ariftus advifed the whole party to abandon the flaring fcene, and to refrefh their eyes by gazing on the turf in fome fhady place. They did fo, and all went well again. In confequence, it was fettled by her Majefty in council, that, during the fummer, it were better for the leaves of trees to be green than to be rofe colour.

Myra was fo enchanted with the pleafures of her palace, that fhe gave herfelf little trouble as to what paffed in the ifland at large. Her whole time

time was employed in schemes for increasing and varying her amusements: sometimes, indeed, she walked into the country, but her presence no longer appeared to give any pleasure to her subjects,—there were no more songs in her praise— no more cries of " Long live our Queen !"— " What," said Myra, " can occasion this strange " alteration in the behaviour of my people? " Are they displeased with any part of my go- " vernment?"—" If," said Philintus, " they are " out of humour with such an amiable Sovereign, " they do not deserve the honour of her enqui- " ries." This answer was not entirely satisfactory to the Queen; she was, even for some time, buried in thought; but the efforts of Philintus, (who had observed the gloom on her countenance) and the gay turn of his conversation, together with the novelty of an entertainment which he proposed for the next evening, drove away all serious thoughts, and sprightliness resumed its reign again. The plan was, that all the court should appear in pastoral dresses, and that the company should dance on one of those elegant lawns with which the palace garden abounded. Myra approved of this plan, only desiring that the habits might be as elegant as the plan would allow. " They can only be made " of linen, madam," said one of the bedcham- " ber-women. " How so?" said the Queen.

" There

"There is not, in your Majesty's dominions, silk enough for one dress."

"You must be mistaken. On my taking the government into my hands, I observed shops without end, well furnished with silk."

"It is true, Madam, there were such; but they are now all shut up, and the owners have left the island."

"And why so, pray?"

"Since your Majesty's orders for the destruction of all caterpillars, the silk manufacture is entirely stopped."

"Aye! why, what have those nasty vermin to do with the manufacture of silk?"

"There is one species of those caterpillars which produces the materials, without which silk cannot be made; and as the sellers of silk in towns are in general connected, by marriage or relationship, with the breeders of silk-worms, they have determined all together to quit a country where they are deprived of the means of subsisting."

That very evening the Queen observed with a surprise, which almost equalled horror, that the apartments of the palace were lighted with tallow candles. "Heavens!" exclaimed the affronted Sovereign, "what means this filthy sight?" She was told that there were no waxen tapers to be found in the isle. "'Tis impossible!"

"impossible!" she cried; "let Aristus be sent
"for." He appeared. "Have you not told
"me, Sir, that my island abounded with wax?"
"Madam, it did so, when I gave you that infor-
"mation." "And how happens it that it is
"not so now?" "Because since your Majesty
"ordered the bees to be extirpated, no more
"wax is to be found." Philintus sneered at
this reply, and Myra asked with astonishment,
"What was the connection between bees and
"tapers?" "Without them," said Aristus,
"the tapers can not exist, since the bees supply
"the materials of which the tapers are com-
"posed." And what is become of those who
"used to get their living by making those ta-
"pers?" "Poor souls!" replied Aristus, "they
"are on the point of quitting a place, where
"they cannot earn their bread. Alas!" added
he, "were your Majesty to make, at this time,
"the tour of your dominions, you would find
"the face of the whole country deplorably
"altered." Philintus would have turned this
account into ridicule, but Myra, by a look,
stopped his buffoonery, and retired to her
chamber with a heavy heart.

The next morning she took Aristus with her,
and drove into the environs of her capital.
"You were too much in the right," said she,
"when you bad me expect a deplorable altera-
"tion

"tion among my people. I hear no more ac-
"clamations! no more fongs! but I fee the
"painfulleft of fights; crowds of people in rags,
"begging their bread," "Formerly," faid
Ariftus, "no beggars were to be found here;
"there was a large building erected for the poor,
"where the old where maintained, the fick
"cured, and all the young folks fet to work; but
"fince your Majefty has allowed twelve to be
"the age of difcretion, many of thefe children
"have refufed to be employed, and chufing to
"wander about the country, without knowing
"how to get their bread, they are of courfe re-
"duced to rags and mifery."

The Queen, having given fome relief to thefe wretched objects, proceeded to afk Ariftus, what was become of the crowds of bufy people who were ufed to throng in the ftreets of the capital? "for," faid fhe, "half the houfes feem to be
"fhut up, and the whole town appears defert-
"ed, in comparifon of its ftate when I firft faw
"it." The minifter told her, "that there was
"a mutual dependance of one trade upon ano-
"ther, and that, in confequence of the depar-
"ture of the filk and wax merchants and manu-
"facturers, thofe who were ufed to fupply that
"large body of men with cloaths, fhoes and
"ftockings, provifions, and every other accom-
"modation, having now no market for their
"goods,

"goods, had shut up their shops, and were pre-
"paring, one and all, for their departure." He
added, "that it was much to be feared, that
"the farmers, who used to bring to the town
"corn, hay, butter, eggs, poultry, &c. together
"with their families, labourers, &c. would soon
"follow this example."

Struck with this painful detail, the young Queen, whose goodness of heart was equal to the thoughtlessness of her head, exclaimed in an agony of distress, "Oh heavens! why did I
"leave my father's court? why take upon me
"a task of which I was so incapable? I suffer
"severely for my presumption, but at least I
"will do no more mischief here." Then turning to Aristus, she begged him to hasten the preparations for her return to the kingdom of her father. Her orders were instantly obeyed, and she, with her whole court, took leave of the Fortunate Island, and soon reached the port they wished for. As soon as Myra saw the King, she threw herself at his feet, bathed in tears. "How is this," said he, "my daughter, are you re-
"turned already? are you so soon weary of
"sovereign power?" "Alas! Sire!" replied the weeping Myra, "never was any being more
"wretched than your daughter! I have child-
"ishly thrown away my own happiness, and
"that of those whom you entrusted to my care.

"The

"The island which I have governed, no longer
"deserves the name of Fortunate. I have, by
"my own mismanagement, reduced an industri-
"ous people to beggary and ruin! but I con-
"jure you, Sire, to order all my jewels to be in-
"stantly sold, that I may, by their means, in
"some sort relieve the miseries which my in-
"fantine folly has brought upon them." "Make
"yourself easy," said the good King, soothing
his afflicted daughter, "the mischiefs which
"your want of consideration has caused, are by
"no means irreparable. I foresaw that you
"would make great mistakes in government,
"and managed affairs so as to prevent those
"mistakes from having any very bad conse-
"quences. Those of your subjects, who have
"by your errors been forced to quite your isle,
"have, by the direction of Aristus, found a
"comfortable retreat in this kingdom, have
"been supplied with all necessaries, and will
"now return to their own country, with proper
"materials, to re-assume their several trades
"and occupations. You have, my beloved
"Myra, an excellent heart, and in all the mis-
"chief which you have done, you have had the
"best intention in the world. This ought to
"teach you that princes ought not to trust to
"their good dispositions alone, but that they
"should take counsel with the most intelligent
"of

"of their subjects, concerning the measures of
"their government, and above all, that they
"should guard against forming too high an opi-
"nion of their own wisdom. The errors of
"private persons can only affect a small number
"of individuals, but those of sovereigns may
"ruin nations."

Myra profited by this lesson, and by her own experience. She dedicated, for the future, a considerable part of her time to study, and forbad Philintus ever to appear in her presence again. X.

THE ELEPHANT.

NEXT to man, the Elephant is the most respectable of the Almighty's creatures. In size he exceeds all other terrestrial animals; and by his understanding he approaches nearly to the human species. His temper is naturally gentle. Even while wild in the forests he thirsts not after blood, nor does he use his vast strength, except in defending himself or protecting his companions. His favourite food is rice, roots, and herbs; he abhors fish and flesh. When he finds a plentiful pasture, he makes use of a particular cry, which gives notice to his comrades to come and partake of the dainties which he has found.

An invitation which they readily obey, to the great loſs of the owner of the land.—The Elephant is caught and tamed without difficulty. His love of ſociety renders him eaſy to be allured into a ſnare by others of his own ſpecies, who have been educated for that purpoſe. Two of theſe, after he is in confinement, conſtantly attend all his motions, and, when he is not diſpoſed to ſubmit, compel him by ſtriking him with their trunks to obedience. Very ſoon, however, his own aſtoniſhing judgment convinces him that no harm is meant to him, and that his efforts towards reſiſtance are all in vain. In conſequence of this he applies himſelf to learn his duty, and becomes the mildeſt and moſt obedient of all domeſtic animals. He ſoon learns to comprehend ſigns. He diſtinguiſhes the tone of command, of anger, and of approbation. He never miſtakes the voice of his maſter, receives his orders with attention, and executes them with prudence and eagerneſs, but without precipitation. He ſeems to take pleaſure in being covered with gilded harneſs and gay houſings. He draws carriages, waggons, artillery, &c. with evenneſs and good humour, provided he be not treated ill, undeſervedly, and that the people who are employed with him have the air of being pleaſed with his behaviour. His conductor (ſtyled his Cornac) generally rides on the

the Elephant's neck, and carries in his hand a sharp iron, with which, when necessary, he pricks the creature's head or ears, to make him move faster; but this is seldom put in practice, since words are always sufficient, provided that the Cornac has had time to acquire the Elephant's confidence; after which the beast's attachment and affection become so strong, that one is actually recorded to have died of grief, because in a fit of passion he had killed his keeper.

Before the invention of gunpowder, Elephants were used in war, and have often by their efforts decided the fate of battles. On their backs they carried small towers which held five or six armed men; and from their trunks hung heavy chains, which they were taught to swing around them in order to break the ranks of the enemy's army. But now that fire is the chief instrument of death in battles, the Elephant, as he is subject to dread both the noise and the flame of fire-arms, would be dangerous to his own party. He is still employed by Europeans in the east for the purpose of transporting the baggage of their troops, and by the Indian princes, for carrying their women in large cages covered with green branches of trees.

Elephants are more numerous in Africa than in Asia, the only two parts of the world where they are, naturally, found. In Africa they live uncontrouled,

uncontrouled, for they defpife the negroes as a fet of unfkilful, weak beings, who have neither ftrength nor art enough to reduce them to flavery. Thofe of the Afiatic ifland, Ceylon, are looked upon as the largeft, boldeft, and moft intelligent of the whole fpecies.

The Elephant is ftrong in proportion to his vaft bulk. He can with eafe carry from three to four thoufand weight; and on his tufks alone he can fupport upwards of one thoufand pounds. The quicknefs of his paces, when the immenfe weight of his body is confidered, is a proof of his amazing ftrength. His ufual walk equals the common trot of a horfe; and he can run as faft as a horfe can gallop. He is generally permitted to walk when loaded, and can with eafe perform fifty miles in a day, but, when pufhed, can go almoft twice as far. He will do as much work as fix ftrong horfes, but his price is immenfe, and the charge of maintaining him very great indeed. An Elephant who has been properly difciplined is worth from four to twelve hundred guineas; and he will eat in a day above a hundred pounds of rice, befides vegetables. In India all barrels, facks, and bales of goods are carried from place to place by Elephants, and if their necks and trunks have no more room for burthens, they will carry an additional weight in their mouth. The Elephant unites fa-

F gacity

gacity with strength, and never injures any thing committed to his charge, be it ever so delicate. He will carry each particular parcel to a boat in his trunk without wetting it; he will range each in order, will try whether each lies firm, and will actually place stones where necessary to prevent casks from rolling from their proper stations.

The trunk (or proboscis) of this wonderful animal ought to be particularly described. It extends itself considerably beyond his mouth, and is terminated by a protuberance which performs all the offices of, and is by no means unlike to, a finger; with this he can lift the smallest piece of money from the ground; he can untie knots; he can turn keys, push back bolts, or loosen straps from buckles; and with this he can gratify his sense of smelling (which there is reason to believe to be very exquisite) by gathering flowers, and conveying them to his nose, which, as well as his finger, composes a part of his trunk. The orange tree, in whose flowers he delights, both for their taste and smell, is an object of his most eager pursuit.

The Elephant, when old, suffers great inconvenience from the increasing size of his large teeth or tusks; to remedy this evil, his natural sagacity prompts him to make two holes in a tree, if wild, or if tamed, in a wall, to support them,

them, and prevent the vaſt fatigue which his neck endures from their weight. As great part of his ſkin is tender and delicate, he ſuffers much from the bites and ſtings of flies. To prevent this inconvenience, he puts in practice all the means which his peculiar good ſenſe ſuggeſts: if he cannot keep the inſects away by bruſhing them off with branches of trees and whiſps of ſtraw, he then wets all the moſt expoſed parts of his body, and gathering duſt with his trunk, ſpreads it carefully over each unguarded place.

The height of the creature in his natural ſtate is generally between ten and fourteen feet; but in captivity his growth is conſiderably checked.

He is nice in many particulars, abhors bad ſmells, and, probably on that account, dreads the fight or even the cry of a hog. In eating, let him be ever ſo hungry, he will faſt until he has nicely examined his victuals, and ſeparated from them every particle of dirt, duſt, or other uncleanlineſs.

Both antient and modern writers dwell with peculiar pleaſure on the innumerable inſtances of inſtinct, or rather ſomewhat which approaches very nearly to reaſon, in this noble animal; but of theſe we ſhall ſelect a few of the beſt atteſted.

An Elephant had been provoked by ill uſage

to kill his conductor.—The widow, who had been a witness to the horrid scene, rushed with her two infant children to the enraged animal. —" Here," said she, " since you have slain my " husband, take my life too, and complete your " bloody business by destroying these poor " babes!" The beast, apparently hurt at his own excess of passion, lost at once his resentment, and taking the eldest of the children in his trunk, adopted him, as it were for his governor, and would never suffer any other person to mount his neck.

If the Elephant is revengeful when ill treated, he is truly grateful to those who use him kindly. A soldier in the East Indies had been accustomed, when he received his pay, to treat one of these sensible animals with arrack; one day, having himself partaken too largely of the same liquor, he escaped from a detachment who had been ordered to convey him to prison, and taking shelter beneath the creature whom he had obliged, he fell fast asleep. His pursuers finding that the Elephant had taken him under his protection, left him, and he, when he awoke, sober, and frightened at his situation, was consoled by the caresses of the good-natured animal, who seemed sensible of the terrors which his benefactor felt, and willing to remove them. An Elephant, in a battle fought not many years ago, having been driven to distraction by the

p ain

pain of his wounds, ran about the field making the moſt hideous cries. A wounded ſoldier of his own party lay juſt in his way, and naturally expected inſtant deſtruction. But the poor tortured animal, conſcious that he owed none of his pain to the ſoldier, took him tenderly up with his trunk, and, having placed him out of the common path, continued his route. This anecdote points out the ſpecies of excellent reaſoning in the Elephant, which prevents him from being provoked, even by the moſt acute pain, to hurt ſuch as have not injured him: but he muſt not be wantonly inſulted; and even the moſt trifling affront may expoſe the giver to a fatal recompence. An Elephant which was kept at Verſailles* not many years paſt, appeared to know when he was mocked by any perſon, and ſeldom failed to revenge the inſult. A man deceived him, by pretending to throw eatables into his mouth. The animal took this opportunity to knock him down with his trunk, and treated him ſo ſeverely, that he ſcarcely eſcaped with life. Another time a painter, in order to draw him with his trunk elevated, employed his ſervant to throw, or pretend to throw, fruit into the Elephant's mouth; the deceitful

---

* A palace about ten miles from Paris, where the King of France has a collection of curious beaſts, birds, &c. &c.

part of this order was resented by the creature with such excellent sagacity, that instead of revenging himself on the servant, (who appears to have been within his reach) he squirted such a quantity of water from his trunk at the master, (whom he judiciously discerned to be the contriver of his mortification) that it utterly ruined the paper on which his work was going forward.

It is recorded, and universally credited, of an Elephant, that as he was passing along a street in the city of Delhi, he thrust his trunk in at the window of a room where a taylor sate, employed on a rich habit.—This man, displeased at being interrupted in his work, caused the animal to withdraw in great haste, by pricking him with a needle; provoked at this treatment, the Elephant, who knew that he should pass by the same street again the next day, it being the usual road to his watering place, took care to be prepared for his enemy, by laying in a store of dirty water; this he emptied from his trunk at the same window, and completed his revenge, by thoroughly spoiling the silk on which the taylor was at work.

Accounts hardly credible, although perfectly well attested, are told of the Elephant's sensibility to reproach. One in particular, having been upbraided by his keeper, as a poor indolent creature, for having failed in an effort to set

afloat

afloat a veffel which lay afhore, an attempt which was really beyond his ftrength, was fo much hurt by the charge, that he made a new trial, fucceeded in it, but fell inftantly dead, from the damage which he had received in confequence of the exertion.

It has been faid before, that mild as the Elephant naturally is, he is not to be trifled with. One of thefe animals having, with great fagacity, carried the iron veffel in which he ufually drank, to the fmith's fhop where it ufed to be repaired, the workman mended it but by halves; the Elephant carried it back, and was feverely reproached by his mafter, who made him comprehend, by fhewing him how the water ran out of the veffel, that it needed a farther repair. The animal, as much hurt as if *he* had been accountable for the workman's neglect, fnatching the veffel out of the owner's hand, half full of water as it was, carried it in hafte to the fhop, and as foon as the perfon who had done his work fo ill appeared, the Elephant difcharged the water in his face, as a punifhment for his mifbehaviour.

Hitherto, M. Buffon has fupplied what has been faid of the Elephant; what follows, is chiefly taken from Sparman's account of the Cape of Good Hope.

A female Elephant loft her young one. It feems that it had fallen into the hands of a party of the native Hottentots, who had killed and devoured it. The mother, the next night, having some how (probably by the scent) discovered the place of its death, attacked the kraal or village in the dark, and utterly destroyed it, by beating down all the huts, and trampling all the plantations to pieces. And here it may be properly remarked, that the Hottentots eagerly seek the flesh of the Elephant to eat it, which is not the case with any other African or Asiatic people, that we read of.

In the country round the Cape, the Elephant is pursued, not to be tamed, but to be slain for the sake of the ivory which his teeth afford. In this chace the danger to the hunter is great; but the hopes of a large profit (sometimes as much as 300 gilders, or about twenty-six pounds, by a single Elephant) make him close his eyes to all perils. He must be very attentive to approach the animal on the side whence the wind blows; for, should he be discerned by his piercing scent, the Elephant rushes on him, nor can any thing save him, except a steep hill or wood, either of which circumstances encumber the beast, and save the sportsman. The bullet which is destined to destroy this immense creature, must be made of a proportionable mixture of tin and lead; the piece from whence it is discharged, is generally one of those musquets which were in use

use about one hundred and eighty years ago, so strong and heavy, as to require a rest to support it when levelled. And yet, when these enormous pieces are deeply loaded, and supplied with proper balls, an Elephant has been known to receive eight wounds in his body before he was deprived of life.

THE THREE SISTERS.

NOT many years ago, there returned from Bengal a man whom we will call John Sterling: he had been well educated, was sprung from a decent family, and brought home the same good heart which he carried out with him from Britain. As his fortune was now very large, and he had formed no matrimonial connections, his first care, on his arriving in his native land, was to discover what relations he had still remaining, and to enquire into their circumstances, in order to bestow on the most deserving of them part of his great acquisitions. It chanced that the person to whom he applied was able to assist in his search. " Some, at least," said he, " of your family I can give you a pretty good " account of: you have two cousins settled in " London ; they are sisters, and are by no means " in distressed circumstances, but are perfect " contrasts.

"contrasts to each other in their manner of living. The eldest of them is avaricious to an extreme, lives in a paltry lodging, keeps but one maid servant, and, in short, seems to have no pleasure on earth, except that of heaping up money. Not so her younger sister; she takes care to spend to the very extremity of her income. She takes great delight in dress, equipage, and every species of luxury, but her expences of the showy kind never prevent the exertions of her humanity: there passes no week in which she does not distribute, on an appointed day, money, cloaths, and victuals, to a number of beggars, who crowd around her door to be relieved."—"This last cousin of mine," said our Indian, "I like well enough, by your account; but as to the other, not a penny of mine shall she have, to add to her heaps, an old avaricious skin-flint!"

With these sentiments, John Sterling set out to visit his youngest relation. From her he met with a polite and hospitable reception, and departed from her house in a perfect good humour with her and her manner of living.

It happened that the only maid servant who lived with the elder sister, was acquainted in the family of the person from whom Sterling had received his intelligence concerning the characters of the two sisters. Some of the domestics had

had overheard the conversation, and took the first opportunity to reproach the girl for the parsimony of her mistress, which they told her had lost her the sharing of a fine sum of money. This soon reached the ears of the female miser, whose vexation, at hearing what she had missed, was almost insupportable. The large fortune, which by dint of the most penurious œconomy she had scraped together, now appeared to her less than nothing, when she considered the immense treasures of her cousin, all of which she thought might have been her own, had she but managed so as to gain the good graces of the owner.— "Perhaps," said she to herself, "it may not, "even now, be too late to retrieve my error. "Some of my money I must sacrifice, it is true, "but then if I succeed, I shall be nobly reim- "bursed. It will go to my heart, indeed, to "part with what has been the whole joy of my "life to procure, but I see no other chance in "my favour, and this scheme must be tried." Having taken her resolution, she determined, as the first step, to contrive to fall into company with her opulent relation. This she soon brought about, by meeting him at her sister's, where he was almost always to be found. She now endeavoured, by every winning grace in her power to captivate his attention, and when she thought she had in some measure succeeded, she took an

opportunity to reproach him for appearing to have forgotten that he had such a relation as herself. "No, Madam, said the blunt Sterling, "I had by no means forgotten you, but the plain "truth is, that finding on enquiry, that your "turn and mine were as widely different as light "and darkness, I thought that no good could "arise from any connection between us."— "I comprehend you, Sir," replied the lady, "you have heard me represented in the most "odious colours, as a pattern of meanness and "avarice. How cruel is the tongue of defama- "tion! I have laid up money, it is true, but "Heaven knows with what intent! The service "of my indigent fellow-creatures has been my "real motive, and it was only to amass a sum "sufficient to lay the foundation of a new hos- "pital, that I have deprived myself of not only "the *superfluities*, but almost of the *necessaries* "of life. At length I have attained to my wish, "and to-morrow I intend to deposit, in the hands "of proper trustees, five hundred guineas, which "I mean to be laid out in the purchase of land "for the edifice to stand upon." The honest Indian was completely taken in by this ma- nœuvre. "How unjustly," said he to himself, "have I thought of this poor woman! Here has "she denied herself every gratification for the "sake of the poor, and I have looked on her as
"a self-

"a self-interested miser! Well, well, I must contrive to make her amends." Then turning to the lady, "Madam," said he, "hitherto I have mistaken your character, but I now honour you as much as a few hours past I despised you. But you must not prevent me from sharing with you the merit of the noble work which you have taken in hand; to-morrow I will attend upon you, and will add my part to the donation which you are about to make." He kept his word, and accompanied her the next morning: he then saw her make a deposit of the sum which she had mentioned, to which he joined a much more considerable present for the same charitable purpose.

The worthy Sterling was recounting the adventures of the day to his friend, and was telling him how very unjustly he had thought of the elder of his cousins, when he was told that an old domestic of the family earnestly entreated to speak with him. "Perhaps," said the good East-Indian, "he may need my assistance; let him come in." The poor fellow entered. "Can I, my good friend, be of any service to you?" said Sterling. "I am very unfortunate," said the suppliant, "and it is only the report which I have heard of your goodness, that has tempted me to this application. I lived twenty years in the service of your worthy uncle: I mar-
"ried

"ried, and when I loſt my good maſter, I ſet up
"a little ſhop: when I was going on with tole-
"rable ſucceſs, I was utterly ruined by an unfor-
"tunate fire, which conſumed my whole ſtock.
"Since that cruel event, I have been unable to
"provide for my young and numerous family,
"and I now preſume to hope that your good-
"neſs will enable me to put my poor children
"into ſome way of buſineſs."

"But why, in the name of wonder, did you
"not apply to my two couſins!" "Alas, good
"Sir, I addreſſed myſelf to them in the begin-
"ning of my misfortunes; but from the eldeſt I
"met with a poſitive refuſal; and the other
"lady, though ſhe offered me ſome relief, yet
"ſhe accompanied that offer with the condition
"of my coming publicly along with the other
"poor, to receive charity at her door; and in-
"deed, Sir, it appeared hard to one who had
"been a reputable tradeſman, to be reduced to
"beg his bread at a door in a public ſtreet. No,
"Sir, I rather choſe to get into a ſervice, which
"I fortunately contrived to do."

"And what, my good friend, became then of
"your children?"

"My eldeſt daughter, Sir, has had the happi-
"neſs of being protected by your Honour's cou-
"ſin, Madam Sophia, who is goodneſs itſelf,
"and who, although in very narrow circum-
"ſtances,

"stances, yet finds opportunities of doing a
"thousand good actions."

"How!" said the good Sterling, "and have
"I another cousin? And is she poor, and yet is
"she charitable? And have I, like a blockhead
"as I am, been ignorant of her very existence?"

"There is such a one, I assure you, Sir; she
"is the daughter of your uncle, and the youngest
"of the three sisters."

"Is this possible?" said the East-Indian, and
"if so, how comes it about that neither of her
"sisters have mentioned her name to me?—
"Where has she lived? How came she so poor?"

"The good lady, Sir, trusted her fortune in
"the hands of a merchant, who became a bank-
"rupt, and lost nearly the whole of it. She
"then retired, with what little she had remain-
"ing, to a village in the country, where she
"boarded at the house of a friend of her's, who
"married a clergyman. There, from her small
"income, she found means to be of infinite ser-
"vice to her poor neighbours; she visited the
"sick, she instructed the young, and, by her ex-
"ample and advice, she reclaimed the idle, and
"encouraged the worthy members of society.
"As to her name not being mentioned to you by
"her sisters, I fear their motive for keeping you
"in ignorance concerning her, was their con-
          "sciousness

"sciousness of her superior claim to your favour
"and protection."

"This," cried Sterling, "is the exact person
"that I am looking for. Come, my lad, get
"your boots ready, to-morrow you shall be my
"guide to the village where this precious cousin
"of mine resides; trouble yourself no more
"about your children; they shall henceforward
"be *my* care: and as to yourself, quit your ser-
"vice as soon as you can with decency; you are
"too old to wear a livery, I will provide for you
"comfortably for the rest of your life."

"Oh, Sir," said the old servant, "be assured
"that what is left of that life shall be employed
"in praying for blessings on you, and on my
"kind benefactress, Madam Sophia."

Sterling soon reached the village. He alighted at the parsonage, and enquired of the minister concerning his amiable cousin. "She is an an-
"gel," said the priest; "notwithstanding the
"loss of her fortune, her countenance expresses
"the happy tranquillity of her mind. Nothing,
"in short, can deprive her of her benevolence,
"and that benevolence must always insure her
"tranquillity."—"Tell her, I entreat you, Sir,"
said Sterling, "that a relation, whom she has
"never seen, begs to be introduced to her."—
Sophia received her cousin with unaffected regard

gard and natural politeness. "I am enchanted with you, my sweet cousin!" said the East-Indian. "In your modest, neat, linen gown, you look more like a woman of fashion, than your showy sister in her gayest dresses; and poor as you are, your features are illuminated by an air of content which never appears on the visage of that other sister of yours; that rich lady that founds hospitals! But tell me now honestly, cousin Sophy, how has it happened that neither of my cousins ever made mention of your name to me since my arrival? Have you fallen out with them? Or do they not know where you reside?"

"Believe me, Sir," replied Sophia, "I love them both too well to keep them in ignorance of my place of abode, and within these last three days I have written to each of them."—"Hard-hearted wretches!" exclaimed the good Sterling; "can I ever forgive their indifference to so amiable a relation?" "Excuse them this one time," said the gentle Sophia; "I doubt not but that they meant to have made me amends for this omission, by the future kindness of their behaviour." "—No, no," said her cousin, "I know the vileness of their hearts. They were conscious of your superior merit, and dreaded, lest I should reward it by bestowing on you that

"fortune

"fortune which each of them already grasped
"as her own: but their odius cunning and
"greediness shall be disappointed. To your
"ostentatious sister I will not give one farthing;
"she does good, indeed, but it is merely for
"the sake of being talked of abroad as a wo-
"man of unbounded charity. Your penurious
"sister I am still less disposed to encourage.
"The donation which she has made in favour
"of the poor, has her own interest so immedi-
"ately in view, that it gives me infinitely more
"*disgust* than *pleasure*. *You*, my worthy cou-
"sin, who do good actions merely because it is
"right and fitting do to them, *you* I declare to be
"my sole inheritrix; and from this moment I
"insist on your making use of my fortune as if
"it were your own. I know that fortune is by
"no means necessary to your happiness; but I
"know, at the same time, that *your* being rich
"will be the means of communicating happi-
"ness to numbers of sufferers, whom, until now,
"you could only pity and not relieve."

X.

THE CONTRAST.

FREDERIC was the son of a lady of fortune, who, having retired to her estate in
the country, bestowed most of her time on his
education.

education. In return for her attachment to him, Frederic was modest, studious, and humane; he felt the obligations which he was under to his parent, and did his best to requite them by pursuing her instructions with care, and by preferring her company to that of any other person. Jacob, a lad of the same age with Frederic, and whose mother's cottage stood near the park-pale of the lady we have just spoken of, was in every respect of a character directly opposite to that of his amiable neighbour. He was loved by no one, not even by his poor mother, all whose endeavours could never prevail on him even to take the pains of learning to read. The most innocent way in which he spent his time was in loitering from place to place, and lounging about; at other seasons he was the plague of his comrades, and, in consequence, the detestation of the village. Frederic was too well bred up to chuse so vile a boy for a play-fellow; Jacob, however, taking advantage of the opportunities which the situation of the mother's tenement gave him, stole, one day, into the room where Frederic's play-things were kept, broke to pieces his violin and his chariot, completely spoilt his bird organ, and carried off in triumph his hobby-horse.

The author of this mischief was soon discovered; and Frederic, in the first emotions of resent-

resentment, was running by the advice of a servant, to acquaint the mother of Jacob with the exploits of her son, "But, no," said he, checking his speed, "she is a severe woman, and she "will horsewhip him without mercy, and, may "be, shut him up in an out-house for a week "together: How should I like that for my- "self? No, no, I had better forgive him, for "this once."

Not long after this, Frederic was walking out with his beloved mother, when unluckily they strolled near a place where the thoughtless, wicked Jacob was amusing himself by throwing stones with all his little force at every object within his reach, totally regardless of the mischief which he might occasion. One of these unluckily hit the little Frederic on the head, and fetched the blood; but Frederic was too much of a man to cry at a little pain.— "Mama," said the spirited lad, "this stone has "hurt me a little, but I dare say the pain will "soon be over." As his forehead, however, was all covered with blood, his mother went directly home with him, and had every proper care taken of his wound. It was an ugly one, and brought on a fever, and it was the end of seven or eight days before he was permitted to walk out, and his mother being engaged with company, ordered a servant to accompany him.

As

As they were walking, the discourse turned on the wickedness of Jacob; and just as the domestic was hoping they might see nothing of him during their walk, they heard a rustling noise in a tree behind them, and down, at once, came Jacob, screaming and crying, from the top of an elm, which his usual spirit of mischief had tempted him to climb in pursuit of a crow's nest. " I fear," said Frederic, exerting his utmost endeavours to raise the poor wretch, " that you " have hurt yourself sadly." Jacob still continued his groans and cries; and well he might, for, upon examination, his leg appeared to be broken in two places. " Poor fellow," said the benevolent Frederic, " how he must suffer! let " us contrive some how or other, to convey him " home to his mother.—Unhappy woman! " what distress must she not feel when she sees " the condition of her unlucky son!" Her distress was great indeed. " Poor as I am," she exclaimed, " I can just support myself and this " ungracious lad; but how shall I ever be able " to pay the long demand which the surgeon " will have upon me, by the time that Jacob " recovers." Little Frederic, who was a witness to her complaints, afforded to them those tears which his own suffering could never extort from him.—" Make yourself easy, my good " neighbour," said the amiable boy, "and oblige
" me

" me so far as to accept this new crown-piece,
" which my good Mama has just given me, that
" I might buy me a fairing, but I can do with-
" out it better than *you* can." The afflicted
mother looked at him with silent admiration.
Frederic proceeded to assure her, that as he was
conscious of the smallness of the sum, (though
it was his all) he would use his interest with his
parent for a larger supply, and did not doubt to
obtain it. The unfortunate woman now found
her tongue, and expressed in the most affecting
terms, her astonishment at seeing his earnestness
in relieving that worthless lad, by whose mischievous hand his forehead was *still* smarting.
" This," said she, " is *truly* to return good for
" evil!" Frederic now returned to his mother,
and after giving her the history of the whole
occurrence, " How comes it, Mama," said he,
" that although I was truly sorry for poor Ja-
" cob's misfortune, and though I feel both for
" him and his mother, yet, on the whole, I am
" more *pleased* than *grieved*?" Child," said the
lady, " you have had an opportunity of doing
" well, and you have made use of it; and, be-
" lieve me, throughout life you will find, that
" the consciousness of having done a benevolent
" action will be the most effectual cordial for
" every painful sensation."

THE

THE NATURAL HISTORY OF THE LION.

THE Lion, though inferior in ſize to ſeveral other animals which inhabit the ſame countries with himſelf, is ſo ſuperior in the united qualities of ſtrength, addreſs, and courage, as to have obtained the higheſt rank amongſt the brute creation. Even the cumbrous Elephant, and the robuſt Buffalo, are conquered by this lordly beaſt, who proudly ſubdues and preys upon all, but is himſelf the prey of none. Nor is his courage leſs remarkable than his ſtrength. The fierce Lion, who has been uſed to conquer, and is ignorant of the ſuperior powers of man, will ſometimes ruſh upon a caravan which is travelling through the deſerts; and ſuch is his contempt of danger, that when he is repulſed, he does not turn his back, and endeavour to eſcape, but retreats fighting, and defending himſelf againſt the attacks of his enemies. The largeſt Lions are about eight or nine feet in length, and three or four feet in height: their colour is yellow on the back, and a duſky white on the ſides and belly. The male Lion is adorned with a large flowing mane, which grows larger as he advances in years; but the female is without this ornament, and is about one-fourth leſs in ſize. In general the Lioneſs
is

is much more docile and gentle than the Lion; but when she has young, she becomes still fiercer than he, and will attack a number of armed men in defence of her whelps. Her care to secure them from discovery is shewn before their birth; she retires to the least frequented places, and when they are brought forth, she is so careful to preserve them, that when she leaves them to procure food, she carefully brushes away the marks of her feet with her tail, that her young may not be discovered by the prints of her steps. The Lion is an inhabitant of warm climates, and is never found in the frozen regions of the North. Indeed the strength and fierceness of this terrible animal appear to be greatly increased by the heat of the climate he inhabits; and there is a remarkable difference between the ferocity of those Lions which breathe the temperate air of lofty mountains, and of those which dwell in the sandy and scorching plains. The American Lions, which are natives of a milder climate, have neither the fierceness, the strength, nor the courage of those born under the fervid rays of an Indian or African sun; nor are they adorned with a mane. Indeed, their differing in so many respects has made several Naturalists very doubtful whether or not they were of the true Lion species.

Though the Lion is naturally an inhabitant of
hot

hot countries, he can fubfift a long time in more temperate climates. Several have lived during many years in Europe, and fome have brought forth young, and attained to a confiderable age, in England. The time which has been fuppofed the ufual term of their lives is between twenty and twenty-five years. Their numbers have been greatly leffened by the increafe of the human fpecies, and the invention of fire-arms; and though many ftill inhabit the fouthern parts of Africa and Afia, and are very fierce and dreadful, yet they are no longer found in very large numbers. Thofe Lions which dwell near the villages of India or Barbary, have fo often proved the fuperior powers of man, that they have loft much of their native fiercenefs, and, if forced by hunger, or provoked by the attacks of men, they attempt to affault them, they approach with great caution and figns of fear. It is however afferted, that if this fierce beaft has conquered, and has once tafted human flefh, he will never afterwards prey with equal pleafure upon any other animal.

When the Lion prepares to attack his prey, he generally makes ufe of ftratagem to enfure his fuccefs. He lies in wait near the fprings where the animals go to drink, couched upon his belly, darts upon them as they pafs, and feldom miffes his aim, though he frequently makes

a leap

a leap twelve or fifteen feet in length. As he neither hears nor sees very well, though he has the faculty of seeing in the night, he is known to employ great watchfulness to procure his prey, and is obliged to keep at a considerable distance from the animal he means to attack, who would, if he came nearer, soon discover him by his strong scent. Springs and fountains are very agreeable to him, not only on account of their being frequented by other animals, but also from the great thirstiness of the Lion; for though he is able to support great hunger, he suffers much from thirst. When he attacks the Buffalo, he rushes upon him unseen, fastens his two fore paws upon his mouth and nostrils, and does not resign his hold till the animal is quite strangled; he then sometimes tears out the entrails that he may remove the body with more ease, and drags it to a retreat, where he may enjoy his feast in security.

All animals appear to have a natural dread of the Lion, and travellers have frequently been acquainted with their approach by the uneasiness of their cattle. The oxen and horses sigh deeply, and shew every appearance of terror, and the dogs creep close to the feet of their masters, and are afraid even to bark. At the sound of his terrible voice the affrighted animals run wildly about to avoid him; but as he lays his

mouth

mouth to the ground when he utters his deep continued roars, the sound is so diffused, that they know not whence it proceeds, and they frequently advance to the very spot where he stands ready to devour them. But terrible as the Lion is to every other animal, he is so inferior to man, that he is not only frequently taken in toils, which are formed to destroy him, but is even hunted for amusement. The inhabitants of the southern parts of Africa, mounted on horseback, frequently pursue and kill him, and they esteem his flesh both pleasant and nourishing. His skin, which in some countries has been used as a royal mantle, is however regarded as very inferior in real usefulness to the hide of an ox.

The inhabitants of the Cape of Good Hope, who are much infested by Lions, which devour their flocks, make use of many artifices to destroy them. In travelling in the night, they are obliged to be pretty constantly upon their guard against this fierce animal, though he seldom attacks them in the day, except he is very hungry, or greatly provoked. A Hottentot, who was travelling to a considerable distance, observed that he was followed by one of these formidable animals, which kept several yards behind him, but advanced with exactly the same speed. Sensible of the cunning of the Lion, who seldom attacks his prey openly, the traveller concluded

cluded that he only waited for the approach of darkneſs to ruſh upon him; and as he was without weapons, and at a great diſtance from any habitation, he was in the utmoſt danger of being torn in pieces by his purſuer. His knowledge of the manners of the animal, and his own ingenuity, furniſhed him, however, with the means to eſcape. He carefully ſought for ſome rocky place, which was level at the top, and had a deep precipice on one ſide; and ſeating himſelf on the brink, he prepared for the part he was to act to ſave himſelf from deſtruction, while his enemy lay couched upon the ground, and ſteadily obſerving him. As ſoon as it became duſk, the Hottentot, gently ſliding forwards, let himſelf down upon a ſmall part of the rock which projected juſt below him; and which was juſt large enough to ſupport him; but in order to deceive the Lion, he raiſed his ſtick, upon which he had placed his hat and cloak, and made a gentle motion with it juſt above his head, at a ſmall diſtance from the edge of the mountain. This ſtratagem had the deſired ſucceſs. The Lion crept gently towards the ſtick, which he miſtook for the man, and then bounded upon it, with ſo exact an aim, as to fall down the precipice cloſe to the ſpot where the Hottentot had placed the ſnare.

There are few diſpoſitions ſo ſavage, that they may

may not be tamed by kindnefs, and even the ferocious Lion has afforded the ftrongeft proofs of attachment and gratitude for the benefits he has received. The celebrated Earl of Peterborough, when a boy, was prefented with a young Lion, which he greatly delighted to carefs and to feed; and the animal became fo tame, as to fuffer his Lordfhip to play with him with the familiarity of a brother. They grew up together, and their intimacy had continued feveral years, when the Earl was appointed by Queen Ann to the command of her army in Spain. His promotion did not, however, make him forgetful of his old friend the Lion; he gave ftrict orders to his houfekeeper to take care of his playfellow. The animal fhewed great concern at the abfence of his Lordfhip, fenfibly pined for his lofs, and refufed his food; and the Earl, in order to preferve his life, ordered him to be prefented to her Majefty, in hopes that the fociety of the other animals in the Tower would make him forget his old friend. A long time paffed before the return of the Earl from Spain, who brought over with him a Spanifh officer whom he had taken prifoner. His humanity made him defirous of making the captivity of the Spaniard as eafy as poffible; and in hopes of amufing him, he took him to view whatever was curious, in or near London, and amongft other places they vifited the Tower. Here the Earl was received by a roar of joy from his old companion, who immediately knew him, and shewed the greatest transports at the return of his benefactor; nor did he suffer him to depart, till, in the excess of his rapture, he had deprived his Lordship of nearly the whole of his coat, though he very carefully avoided injuring his person.

FATAL EFFECTS OF DELAY.

CHARLES STANLEY was the second son of a gentleman, who possessed a small estate in Yorkshire, which at his death was designed for his eldest son, and the youngest was to be brought up to some genteel business, by which he might improve the little fortune which his father intended for him. Charles gave early marks of a sweet and engaging temper; he was dutiful to his parents, he tenderly loved his brother, and was so obliging to the servants, that he became the favourite with them all. Every little boy in the village talked of the good nature of little Charles, and of his willingness to part with his sweetmeats and playthings.

When Charles was about four years old, his father sent him to a neighbouring school, where he was very soon as much remarked for the progress

gress he made in learning as he had been for his sweet temper. He read better than any boy in the school, and whenever he went before his master to spell, he was certain to get the first place. This great quickness gave much delight to his fond parents and his tutor, though they observed that, with all his good qualities, Charles had one capital fault; instead of going directly to school, he would often loiter in the fields till long after the other boys had gone in, and his books were always to be sought for at the very time when he should have taken them to his master.

At a proper age, Charles was placed by his father at a great school, where he no longer found the indulgence to his faults, which he had met with from the village tutor. He was not allowed to defer the morning's task till the afternoon, and it was remarked to him that he was inferior in learning to many who were his juniors in age. Charles was stung with the remark; he knew that he was able to excel, and he resolved that he would at some time take great pains, and obtain the same rank he had held in the village school; but he thought he might defer this till some future time. His work, while he was under the eye of his master, was performed as well, and in less time than that of most of his school-fellows; but the tasks which he had to perform out of school hours were always deferred, and every thing furnished Charles with an excuse for delay, not that he passed his vacant time in play; instead of that, he was often employed in writing exercises for his school-fellows while they were amusing themselves, and his own task was deferred till the morning, when there was little time to perform it well, and he was punished for the faults. Thus poor Charles seldom enjoyed the proper season for play. He was compelled to complete his task when his companions were enjoying themselves in innocent sports, and he was seldom set free from work till they were retiring to rest.

Charles continued in this situation till the age of fourteen, and was every day remarked for his abilities to excel, and for those habits of delay which often destroyed all the advantages he naturally possessed. Mr. Stanley then took him to London, and placed him with a merchant, a friend of his, in the city, to whom he hoped Charles would become so agreeable, as in time to be admitted into partnership with him. In this situation Charles gave the strongest proofs of integrity, sweet temper, and great abilities, but delay attended whatever he undertook; he was not dressed till some hours after he should be at the desk; he did not get to the Custom-house till

till the books were shut, nor appear upon Change till every man of business had deserted it. With more virtues, and greater ability, than almost any man of his acquaintance, he became a general object of ridicule and derision, and when the term of his apprenticeship expired, he found that, with a character which was shaded with only one foible, all intimate connections with him were shunned by the sober part of the trading world.

About this time Charles had the misfortune to lose his father, who bequeathed him such a fortune as entitled him to expect a partnership in some respectable house. But his known habit of delay prevented his friends from making the offer; and though he fully intended to seek such a connection, yet he continued to defer it till he had greatly lessened his little patrimony. His father had introduced him to several friends who might have assisted him greatly, but he had disgusted them by his conduct, by deferring his visits to unseasonable hours, and by protracting them till the repeated yawns of the family informed him that it was time to depart. Charles, who saw himself in a situation where he was very likely to be without either friends or fortune, now resolved to exert himself, and to follow the plan which his father had traced out for his conduct in life. He could not, indeed, meet with an agreeable partnership, but he determined to enter into a mercantile line by himself; and his friends, who were delighted with his exertions, formed such extensive connections for him, that he had the greatest chance of being in a few years one of the richest men in the city. But, alas! his habit of delay had acquired more strength than he was aware of, and his efforts to conquer it were but transient. Charles soon relapsed into his former indolence. He deferred business till he had not time to transact it. He neglected to comply with the orders of his correspondents till the goods they sent for were no longer wanted; and he omitted insuring his vessels, not because he intended to risk the loss, but because, as he did not see them sinking, he thought he might defer the business to some future time. In a short time his business declined, several of his vessels had either been taken or lost, his creditors poured in from every quarter, his property could not answer their demands; and Charles Stanley, whose integrity was respected by all, was hurried to prison, with the conviction that his misfortunes were the consequence of his folly.

In this wretched situation Charles was a prey to sorrow. His heart was melted at the misery which many poor and innocent families must have suffered from his failure; and he thought of the uneasiness he must have given to his mother with agony. Firmly did he resolve, that if he could ever again be established, he would atone by his future diligence for his past misconduct; but where could he look for assistance? His mother had no more than was sufficient for her support; and his brother had already given him whatever he could afford. Charles was sitting alone, reflecting upon the sad situation of his affairs, when he was informed that a gentleman enquired for him below, and in a few moments, he beheld a brother of his mother's, whom the family had believed to be dead, but who was just returned from India with a large fortune. Mr. Hilton was much grieved at the misconduct and misfortunes of his nephew; but was so much affected by his ingenuous account of his past faults, and his resolutions of amendment, that he generously discharged all his debts, and enabled him to appear again amongst his old acquaintance with credit.

Charles, fully sensible of the miseries from which he had been delivered, was very earnest to settle himself in some business which would afford him support; and his kind uncle, who hoped that a new scene would be favourable to his new-formed plans, earnestly advised him to embark for India, promising to return with him, that he might see him well settled. This goodness filled the heart of Charles with the warmest gratitude: he fell at his feet, and declared with tears, that he would exert himself to the utmost to fulfil the commands of his generous benefactor. Every thing was ordered for their departure, and when the time arrived for the sailing of the ship, Mr. Hilton went on board with some goods which were in readiness, leaving his nephew to follow him to the Downs with those which were not quite finished. But delay again appeared in the conduct of Charles; he omitted enquiring after them till an express arrived from Mr. Hilton, with the account that the vessel was to sail the next day, and that he must hasten down immediately. Charles then began to execute the orders which his uncle had left, but was detained so long before he could get the goods, that when he reached the Downs he found the ship had sailed some hours. Almost distracted with this account, and with the thoughts of what his kind uncle must think of his misconduct, he wandered about for some time in the greatest distress, and at length having become almost desperate, he hired a quick-sailing boat, in hopes of being able to overtake the ship. For some time they advanced rapidly, and gained sight of the India ship, and the heart of Charles was alternately agitated by hope and fear. But suddenly the sky was overcast, the sea swelled, the wind roared, and the boatmen

men declared that there was every appearance of an approaching storm, which soon raged around them with the utmost fury. The vessel, which was too light to resist its force, was tossed about at the mercy of the wind and waves, and the only hope the unhappy Charles had of saving his own life, and those of his companions, was by reaching the ship, which they saw at a small distance before them. But they exerted every effort in vain; a great sea broke over the bark, and Mr. Hilton had the misery of seeing it sink for ever into the bosom of the ocean, and to lament the loss of the unfortunate Charles, who, though possessed of such talents as made him loved and admired by all, yet by one unhappy foible was rendered miserable and ridiculous through life, and subjected to a dreadful and premature death.

THE NOSEGAY.

CAPTAIN DORMER, and his amiable Lady, had lived during several years at their seat in Dorsetshire, happy in themselves, and beloved by all around them, when they received the unwelcome account that the Captain was commanded to join his regiment, which was ordered to embark for America. The news of this

this event filled all the country with sorrow. The rich grieved for the loss of so excellent a neighbour; the poor mourned for the departure of their kind and constant benefactor; and the tenants and servants wept aloud at the thoughts of being separated from a master who had always treated them more like children than dependants. But in vain were their entreaties that he would remain; honour called upon him to depart, and Mrs. Dormer saw, with the utmost sorrow, that to honour he would sacrifice the strongest feelings of his breast. She resolved, however, not to be left behind, and in a short time, they exchanged the tranquil pleasures of Belmount for the horrors of carnage and war.

Mrs. Dormer had not been long in America before she lay-in of twins, both daughters, and very beautiful. In the care of these sweet children she found some relief during the frequent absences of her husband, and would often indulge the hope of returning peace, when the Captain, instead of engaging in the slaughter of his fellow-creatures, might enjoy the delight of improving his little Fanny and Sophia. The children daily became more fond of their parents, often clinging to their father when they saw him preparing to go out, and always clapping their little hands with joy when they saw him return. As soon as they were able to speak,

Mrs.

Mrs. Dormer taught them to say Papa, and in a short time, when they saw him at a distance, they would directly leave their play, and running up to their Mama, would cry out, "Papa "is come, dear Papa is come to see his little "girls."

The improvement of the children became more visible every day, and they were daily more dear to their parents, when Captain Dormer, returning from a foraging party, was fiercely and suddenly attacked by the Indians, and a desperate engagement ensued. The time when Mrs. Dormer had expected his return had long passed, and she sat in silent agony looking at her dear children, whom at one moment she feared were deprived of their parent, and the next, stepping to the room door, she anxiously listened to every noise, and was fearful, lest even the sound of her own breath should prevent her from hearing the well-known step of her beloved husband. At length a sound reached her ears—it came nearer; it increased, and she flew down stairs in the fond hope of welcoming the return of what was most dear to her. The door was opened, but it no longer opened to admit the tender husband, and fond father, joyfully returning from the labours of the day;—Captain Dormer was brought in a mangled, lifeless corpse.

Thus

Thus cruelly deprived of her husband, Mrs. Dormer resolved to return to England, and to employ her time in the education of her little girls. She took them down into Dorsetshire, and instructed them herself; and little Fanny and Sophia Dormer were soon remarked as the neatest work-women in the country. But their good Mama did not direct their attention merely to the little arts of making trifling ornaments: she taught them that virtue was superior to accomplishments, and that what was useful was more excellent than what was merely elegant. Little Fanny soon understood, that though music gave her great delight, it was still more delightful by her own sweetness to charm all around her: and Sophia learned that no pleasure was equal to the pleasure of doing good to her fellow-creatures.

In this happy retirement Mrs. Dormer continued for some years improving her sweet girls in real virtue and useful knowledge. At this time Lady Aubrey, a relation of Mrs. Dormer's, paid her a visit, and upon her return would gladly have prevailed with the good mother to suffer both her daughters to spend some time with her in London. This, however, Mrs. Dormer could not agree to; but as Fanny had shewn a strong affection for her ladyship, and earnestly wished to see London, she consented to her going;

ing; and Sophia, who preferred the company of her Mama to any other enjoyment, was left at home. At firſt indeed, ſhe felt uneaſy without her ſiſter; ſhe found a ſolo on the harpſichord was not half ſo agreeable as a duet, and the beautiful alcove in the garden was not near ſo pleaſant, as when Fanny ſat with her there, at her drawing or needle-work. By degrees, however, ſhe became reconciled to her loſs, but frequently thought that Fanny could not enjoy half the pleaſure in London that ſhe did at Belmount, in aſſiſting her Mama to work for the poor people of the village, or in going with her to viſit thoſe who were ſick. But her greateſt delight was in the office which Mrs. Dormer had given her of diſtributing the broken victuals, which were given away to the poor every day at her gate. This was the higheſt pleaſure Sophia could receive. She flew with rapture to the houſe-keeper to obtain her welcome burden, under which ſhe tottered to the door. She exulted in ſeeing ſo many poor creatures made happy by her bounty, and delighted to hear them ſay, " Here comes the good little girl; " ſhe will, one day, be as good a lady as her " Mama;" and ſhe often thought with great pleaſure of the joy which her ſiſter Fanny would have, when ſhe returned, in this new employment.

But

But Fanny's visit to Lady Aubrey unfitted her for the innocent pleasures of Belmount. She never heard of such a thing as working for the poor from her Ladyship; and cards, dress, and elegant equipages, engaged the attention of all the circles to which Fanny was admitted. She almost learned to forget the poor; and when she returned to Belmount, she spoke haughtily to the servants, and scarcely noticed her inferiors; and when the poor came to receive their daily allowance, instead of serving them, she either turned away, or suffered her little favourite dog, Surly, to bark at them, and shake their tattered cloaths. All the village talked of her pride, and lamented that the good Mrs. Dormer should have such a naughty little girl; but the good and gentle Sophia was loved by them all. They presented her with the choicest flowers in their gardens, and the most beautiful bantams and pea-fowls were sent to the poultry yard of the good little girl that behaved so well to every one. When Mrs. Dormer came from church, all the farmers and their wives made their best bows and curtsies to the good lady, who spoke kindly to them all. She was followed by Fanny, who never turned her head aside; but when Sophia came near, the children plucked one another, and said, "Here comes the young lady,

" see

"see how good humoured she looks: she will
"ask us all how we do."

Fanny could not avoid seeing how disagreeable her pride made her to every body, and she found herself much less happy than she was before she went to London; but she had learned there to think that such behaviour was right, and, if it was an error, she foolishly resolved rather to adhere to it than to own she had been wrong. She was one day invited with her sister to a ball at the house of a lady in the neighbourhood, where she was to meet all the young people in that country. Her heart exulted in the thoughts of this gay party, and she resolved to behave in the same manner she had seen some fashionable ladies do in London. Upon entering the room she advanced to a small knot of young ladies of her acquaintance; and, without speaking to the rest of the company, began to make remarks upon their dress and manners in a whispering voice, but in a tone loud enough to be heard. After some time a young lady, whom she had never seen before, entered the room, in a dress made up in a manner very different from any that Fanny had ever observed; she directly began to sneer at her, and declared, that for her part she was surprized such strange figures should think of mixing with people of fashion,

fashion, and wondered where they came from. The young lady confounded at so rude a reception, retired to a corner, where she was joined by the good humoured Sophia, who chatted with her till the lady of the house returned into the room, and introduced her into the company as the eldest daughter of the Duke of Dorset, who was just returned from a tour to France. Nothing could exceed the chagrin of Fanny, when she found that the young lady whom she had been ridiculing was the principal person in the company, and that the dress she had despised, was the admiration of all who saw it. She had not the assurance to endeavour to repair her fault by apologies, or to press her acquaintance upon the lady whom she had so grosly affronted. Indeed she saw that neither her excuses nor intimacy would be accepted, and she had the mortification of hearing her sister Sophia receive a very pressing invitation to Dorset House, in which she was not included.

Fanny was greatly mortified at this incident, and she resolved never to behave in such a manner again. She ought, indeed, directly to have endeavoured to conquer every feeling of pride, and to return to that behaviour which made her beloved by every body; but she only resolved that she would not again laugh aloud at a stranger in a genteel company, and run the
risk

risk of offending her superiors. As to the poor and miserable, she thought them beneath her regard.

Some time after this, Fanny and Sophia were again invited to the house of a lady, whom, as Fanny regarded her as a person of great taste, she was desirous to please her by appearance. She put on all her little finery, but found that one thing was necessary to complete her dress, which was a Nosegay, and this she was determined to buy when they reached the town. They set off in the carriage, attended only by servants, and by Fanny's little dog, which ran at the side of the chariot. Fanny could talk of nothing but of calling at the florist's, and of the elegant Nosegay with which she should be adorned. At length they saw a little tattered girl lying asleep upon the side of the road, whom Surly directly attacked, and began to shake her ragged cloaths. Sophia called him hastily away, and would have succeeded before he had awakened the poor little girl, but Fanny encouraged him to proceed; upon this the child starting up, aimed a blow at the dog, which he avoided, and made a snap at her leg. The poor terrified girl then endeavoured to run away, but in running missed her step, and fell down the bank into the ditch. She had hurt her foot, and lay crying in the ditch till Sophia ordered the

servant

servant to take her up, and, contrary to the advice of Fanny, defired him to place her in the chariot that they might convey her home. She then began to comfort the poor child, and inquired about her hurt; but fhe continued to cry out, " O my poor mammy, my poor mammy, " what will fhe do, now I cannot run about and " beg for her and my daddy!" " Who is your " mammy," faid Sophia, " and what fhall we " do for your foot?" " Oh! don't mind my " foot," faid the child, " give me only fome " bread for my poor mammy and daddy, and " my little brother, and I don't care what be- " comes of my foot."

The child had fcarcely finifhed her fpeech when the carriage ftopped at the door of a cottage, which the little girl faid was her home. When fhe attempted to get out, fhe found herfelf unable to walk, and was obliged to be carried by the footman, who, accompanied by Sophia, entered the houfe, while Fanny remained in the carriage fullenly pouting at her fifter's condefcenfion, and very angry to be fo delayed. She was indeed forry to fee the poor child fo hurt; and when fhe was taken out of the carriage gave her what money fhe could fpare; but fhe took care to keep enough to buy her elegant Nofegay. When Sophia entered the houfe, fhe found a fcene of mifery which fhe could not
have

have conceived. The father of the little girl had long laboured under an ague and fever, her mother was worn down with poverty and fatigue, and her little brother crying for hunger in a corner of a poor cottage, stripped of almost all its furniture, which had been sold to buy necessaries. Sophia found that little Sally had gone out in the morning to beg something for this afflicted family, and that, quite exhausted with hunger and fatigue, she sat down upon the bank and cried herself to sleep. The tender heart of Sophia was greatly affected by this distress; she emptied her pocket of every farthing which it contained, and gave it to the good woman of the house, and would not keep enough to buy the collar which she had once intended for her little favourite squirrel. She then prepared to leave the cottage, but before she went desired the poor people to get what was necessary, and told them she would soon return with her good Mama, who would give them cloaths and victuals enough.

The sisters then proceeded to their visit. Fanny bought her Nosegay, which was very beautiful: but the sweetness of Sophia, and the cheerfulness which the thoughts of the good action she had been performing inspired her with, made her so agreeable, that all the company were charmed with her, but paid little attention to Fanny.

Fanny. At night, when they returned, Mrs. Dormer noticed Fanny's Nosegay, which, though it had begun to fade, was still very beautiful. This pleased Fanny, and she cried out, " Ah! " Mama, I was sure you would like it, it is so " very pretty, and my sister liked it very much " indeed." " Then why did she not buy one?" said Mrs. Dormer; Fanny hung down her head, and in a faultering tone answered, " Because she " had no money." Mrs. Dormer, surprized at this, for she had given some to each of them that very morning, inquired from Sophia what was become of it; Sophia then recounted to her mother the condition in which she had seen the poor people at the cottage, but took care not to mention a word of Fanny's ill behaviour: she then told her the way in which she had disposed of her money, and the promise she had made of taking her Mama to the cottage; and ended by begging that she would go with her in the morning. Transported with her conduct, Mrs. Dormer pressed her virtuous child to her bosom, and promised to take care of the wretched family, for whom Sophia was so much interested. Then looking with anger at Fanny, she said, " Did you then give nothing to these poor " unhappy creatures?" Fanny hung down her head in silence, for she was ashamed to speak; but Sophia said, " O yes, Mama, indeed she

" gave

"gave them all the money she had; except just enough to buy her Nosegay and a trinket for her little watch; and I am sure if she had gone into the cottage and seen their misery, she would have given them that too." "She sat at the door then," said Mrs. Dormer, "while you went in." Then turning to Fanny, "Proud and unfeeling girl," said she, "who could prefer vain and trifling ornaments to the delight of relieving the sick and miserable! Retire from my presence; take with you your trinket and Nosegay, and receive from them all the comforts which they are able to bestow."

Sophia would gladly have retired with her sister; she was grieved at the displeasure she had incurred from her Mama, and she wished earnestly to sooth and comfort the dejected Fanny. Mrs. Dormer, however, chose that she should be left alone, and Fanny was obliged to pass the night by herself. She then began to reflect upon the happiness which she had known before she went to visit Lady Aubrey: she was then beloved by every one, every body met her with a smile; all the servants were ready to oblige her, and all the neighbours loved her; now all was changed, and no one, except Sophia, no, not even her Mama, seemed to love her. At this thought she wept bitterly. "And why am I not beloved?"

beloved?" said she, " And why does every one "shun me, at the very time that they are so "fond of my sister? Alas! it is because I am "not so good as she." Fanny then thought of the vexatious situations into which she had been brought by her vanity and pride. They had caused her to be shunned not only by her inferiors, but by those above her, and had made her generally hated or despised. Heartily ashamed of her conduct, and grieved at its consequences, she passed the greatest part of the night in weeping, and resolving that she would again be good, and again behave in such a manner as should make her beloved by all, and happy in herself.

Towards morning Fanny fell asleep, and, as she was much tired with lying awake so long, she slept till it was pretty late; the next day when she awoke, she inquired for her Mama, and was resolved to ask her forgiveness, and to inform her of her sorrow for her past faults, and her resolution to amend. She was informed that Mrs. Dormer and Sophia were gone to the cottage, and had taken cloaths, and other necessaries for the family, and had sent for a physician to attend the sick man. " Ah!" said she, " Sophia is happy, and she deserves to be "so, for she is good; I was not worthy to "have the pleasure of going to the cottage, "but I will be good and happy too." She then

then rofe, and the firft thing fhe faw was her Nofegay, which the maid had carefully put into a pot of water the night before. "This Nofe-gay," faid Fanny, "fhall be the conftant me-morial of my faults, and of my repentance." She then reached her pallet, and making a beautiful fketch of the almoft dying flowers, fhe wrote under them in a large hand, *Virtue never fades*, and placed the drawing in the moft confpicuous part of the room. When Mrs. Dormer returned, fhe was ftruck with this elegant performance, and calling for Fanny, had the delight of hearing from herfelf what had paffed in her mind during the paft night, and her refolutions of amendment. After fome time, during which Fanny had entirely laid afide her haughty behaviour, the indulgent Mrs. Dormer would have removed the drawing that it might no longer mortify her child; but Fanny begged it might remain, and whenever fhe found herfelf inclined to return to her former folly, fhe placed herfelf before the picture, which foon became, not merely the fhameful memorial of paft faults, but the elegant monument of her return to virtue.

DESCRIPTION OF THE TWO-HORNED RHINOCEROS.

THIS animal is found in Africa, chiefly about the Cape of Good Hope, and is distinguished from the common or one-horned Rhinoceros, as well as from all other beasts, by having two horns upon its nose, the larger of which stands foremost towards the muzzle or snout of the animal, the shorter behind it, and higher up towards the forehead. The foremost horn grows almost to the length of two feet, and seven or eight inches thick at the bottom; the hindmost sometimes measures so long as sixteen inches, and proportionably thick. They are of a conical shape, with the tips inclined somewhat backwards, but their size does not always appear to be in proportion to the body. This species of Rhinoceros is endued with prodigious strength, and, though little inferior in size to the Elephant, and somewhat resembling it in its enormous unwieldy make, runs with astonishing swiftness. It harbours amongst close thickets and bushy copses, from whence it comes forth in the cool of the evening, to graze for the night. Its food consists of plants and roots, with the tops of shrubs, and small branches of trees. The roots it is supposed to dig up with the smaller of its horns, as this, especially in the older animals, is

most

moſt commonly obſerved to be worn away in different parts, which is never the caſe in the foremoſt and larger one. It is natural to ſuppoſe that this latter is the offenſive weapon of the animal, and is therefore never uſed in the ſervile employment of digging for its food, at which time it is turned on one ſide, out of the way; for theſe horns are ſaid to be ſo looſe and moveable, that when the Rhinoceros walks careleſsly along, one may ſee its horns dangle about, and hear them claſh and clatter againſt each other. The ſhrubs and plants, which alſo compoſe part of its food, it clips off with its lips, not having any fore teeth for that purpoſe. Indeed it has little room for them, as the mouth goes off ſo ſharp at the fore part (ſomething like that of Tortoiſe) that it is only an inch and a half broad. Beſides, it has no occaſion for any teeth there, the ſkin which forms the lips being of that extreme hardneſs, that it can perform the office of teeth very well, and that with ſo much the greater eaſe, as the under jaw goes within the upper.

The tongue is perfectly ſoft, which directly contradicts the common notion that the Rhinoceros kills by licking with his tongue.

Notwithſtanding the formidable bulk and amazing ſtrength of this animal, which has been known to run up to a waggon and carry it to a

conſider-

confiderable diftance upon its fnout and horns, the Hottentots and the Dutch farmers who live in the inland parts round the Cape of Good Hope, frequently attack and overpower it. For the purpofe of fhooting it they ufe balls made of lead and tin mixt, and having found out its retirement, they approach it on the fide oppofite to that from which the wind blows. This precaution is abfolutely neceffary on account of the very acute fmell and hearing with which the animal is endued. At the leaft noife more than ufual, it takes the alarm, and erecting its ears, ftands clapping with them and liftening; and if the hunter be fo imprudent as to get to the windward of it, even at a great diftance, it feldom fails directly to follow him by the fcent, and attack him with the greateft fury. Being therefore pretty fecure on the fide of the wind, the Rhinoceros has the fagacity in general to chufe, by way of entrenchment, a bufh very thick, and high on that fide from whence it has no fcent. If wounded it rufhes out from the thickets into the plain, when the boldeft fportfmen prudently confult their fafety by flight. It foon, however, turns afide, and if there be no copfe convenient for its efcape, makes off ftraight forward over the plain: if they happen to have hounds out with them, thefe purfue it, and form a ftrong contraft to the coloffal fize of

the

the animal, which, however, ſeems not to take the leaſt notice of them. With a gentle riſe and fall of the neck it keeps on an even ſteady courſe, a kind of pacing, which neverthelefs gets over a great deal of ground: but this pace, on hearing a few ſhots fired after it, it alters to a faſt gallop, ſo as in an inſtant to leave the hounds at a great diſtance behind; and, in all probability, any ſportſman would inevitably be loſt, who ſhould happen to become the object of its purſuit, if he had not art enough to get out of the ſight and ſcent of it by ſhifting and dodging occaſionally. In this particular the Rhinoceros is ſaid to reſemble the Elephant, that without delaying or ſtopping in the leaſt, it will run to the diſtance of many leagues from the place where it has been cloſely hunted, or in any other way moleſted.

The two-horned Rhinoceros ſleeps in a different poſture from the Elephant: it lies down on the ground on one ſide, and withal is ſaid to ſleep ſo ſound, that the Hottentots and Dutch coloniſts frequently ſteal upon it while in that ſituation, and ſhoot it; it differs very much in this reſpect from the common or one-horned Rhinoceros, which is deſcribed as by no means a ſleepy animal. If it happens not to die immediately of its wounds, the Hottentot hunters will neverthelefs follow the traces of it for one or more days, till it drops down with weakness and fatigue. In general, however, they poison one or two of their darts before they attack it, in which case they have no occasion to wait so many days as they otherwise would before their prey falls into their hands.

Fortunately for those who attack the Rhinoceros, with all its keenness of smell and hearing, it labours under the disadvantage of being extremely near-sighted. In effect, its eyes are very small and sunk into its head, which is perhaps the reason why it sees but indistinctly, and that only straight forward, so as not even to perceive a horseman at the distance of fifty or sixty yards upon the open plain, unless directed by its scent or hearing to fix upon the object. Whenever, therefore, it happens to receive a wound without being able to discover from what hand it proceeds, this circumstance seems to provoke it to a greater degree of fury. Not knowing where to wreak its vengeance, it swings the fore part of its body violently from one side to the other, and snuffs up with its nostrils, as if endeavouring to discover the enemy by its smell. The noise which it makes with its nose upon such occasions is particularly terrible to the horses of those who are in chace of it; for when wounded, it will snuff and blow so hard and so loud as to startle them, and make them uneasy, at the distance

tance of some hundreds of yards. Indeed, instinct sufficiently informs the horse of its danger, when the Rhinoceros is nigh, not only by the hearing but by the smell also; for whenever the sportsmen approach its retreat, which is always done against the wind, the horses having the advantage of the breeze, are enabled to discover their tremendous enemy so far off as forty or fifty yards by the smell: upon this they immediately stop, and give evident proofs of terror by their unwillingness to proceed any farther.

This animal is of a greyish or ash colour, but, which is very remarkable, seems to change its hue, and become almost black upon being hard hunted. This is owing probably to the dust and dried mud that sticks to its skin (as it is very fond of rolling and wallowing in the mire) and when moistened by sweat, becomes much darker in colour. About the groin, however, where the skin is not so thick as on the rest of the body, and almost quite smooth, it is nearly the colour of a man's flesh. On all other parts the surface of the skin is rough and knotty, and not much differing from that of an Elephant, but of a closer texture, and when it is dry extremely hard. It has not, however, any of those plaits and folds which are to be observed in the common descriptions and figures published of it, and which give it the appearance of being covered with a harness. The hide is an inch and a half thick on the back, and somewhat thicker on the sides, though less compact there. It is, however, by no means impenetrable, as has been commonly supposed. Leaden balls, indeed, will sooner be flattened against the skin than pierce it; but when they are hardened by a proper mixture of tin, the Rhinoceros may be killed by a single shot. Nay, its hide, as well as that of the Elephant, is capable of being penetrated by javelins and darts. A Hottentot, at the distance of five or six paces, has been known to pierce through the hide of a Rhinoceros half a foot deep into its body. Some have also imagined it to possess no feeling in its skin; but, besides what is mentioned of the common Rhinoceros, that it is capable of being tickled under the belly with a whisp of straw, the Two-horned Rhinoceros is fond (as was mentioned before) of wallowing in the mire like a hog, which would hardly be the case were its hide absolutely insensible; and indeed, when the thick hide of an Elephant is affected by the stinging of flies, we cannot suppose that of the Rhinoceros to be totally destitute of feeling. Its skin, though tough and close in its texture, has, particularly about the groin, vessels, blood, and juices, adapted for the nourishment of insects; and, in effect, this animal is found to be infested in that part with

a particular

a particular species of insect; neither does the thickness of its hide hinder it from perspiring. Lastly, the Rhinoceros here described may be said to be totally destitute of hair, though there are a few scattered dark bristly hairs, about an inch long, on the edges of the ears, with a very few between and round about the horns, and at the tip of the tail. This part of the animal is about an inch thick, diminishing by degrees from the root to the tip, where it is flattened at the sides; and on the edges, produced by this flatness, are to be seen some strong stiff hairs, an inch or an inch and a half in length. Such of them as stand towards the creature's hard and rough body are visibly worn down and stunted.

Of the inward parts of this animal, it is sufficient to observe, that its flesh, when dressed, tastes a good deal like pork, but much coarser. Its brains are less than those of a middle-sized man; like the horse, it has no gall; its entrails also most resemble those of a horse: so that this beast, notwithstanding its being furnished with horns, does by no means belong to the class of those which chew the cud, but rather of those whose fat is of a soft nature like lard, and not hard like tallow. The stomach, however, does not bear the least resemblance to that of a horse, but rather to that of a man or hog; and the contents of it, when opened, after the animal has

been

been lately killed, are usually without smell, and perfectly fresh and sweet, consisting of roots and small branches of trees chewed, some of them as big as the end of a man's finger; and of succulent plants, the whole diffusing around a very strong and not disagreeable aromatic odour.

THE THREE BROTHERS.

EUGENE, Richard, and Cassander, were the sons of Mr. Smithson, a reputable merchant in the north of England, who having no other children besides them, and being in pretty affluent circumstances, resolved to have them educated immediately under his own eye. For this purpose he invited into his house a Mr. Markham, a gentleman of learning and approved morals, to be their tutor, whose care and attention to their improvement afterwards fully answered all his expectations.

These Three Brothers, from their earliest infancy, were playmates and companions. They had never been sent out of their father's house, either to nurse or even to a school; as Mrs. Smithson, their mother, whose education rendered her perfectly equal to the task, undertook to put them through the first rudiments of learning, and to prepare them for whatever studies

a tutor

a tutor might afterwards direct them to. Whether it was their constant society from their earliest childhood; in the course of which, notwithstanding the difference of two years, between the age of Cassander and that of Eugene, each shared invariably in the studies as well as the amusements of the other two; or whether it was the natural bent of their dispositions, I know not, but they were remarkable for bearing towards each other a degree of affection that is rarely to be found amongst brothers in general. In their sports they were inseparable; the inequality of their number was never an obstacle to their all partaking of the same pastime, though it might originally have been intended but for two; and notwithstanding there would now and then arise a trifling dispute amongst them concerning their play, all differences were usually settled and reconciled before the conclusion of the game, so that they never parted from each other in a pet; but, on the contrary, after they were tired of play, it was no uncommon thing to see them linked all three arm in arm, sauntering up and down the garden walks, which were commonly the scene of their amusements; and in that friendly attitude communicating to each other their little fancies, discussing the remarkable stories that occurred in the course of their

lessons,

lessons, or else laying their heads together to plan and strike out some new mode of diversion.

Thus agreeing, and unanimous in all things, they entered with pleasure upon the course of study laid down to them by Mr. Markham, their tutor. Mrs. Smithson had never, while her sons were under her care, made their lessons a painful

or

or disagreeable task; the novelty, therefore, of Mr. Markham's first examination, under whom they found that they were to learn both Latin and Greek, so charmed and delighted them, that they all three jumped for joy when their Papa shewed them three Lilly's Grammars, which they were to begin the next day. Besides, their satisfaction at not being obliged to leave their dear parents, nor to be separated from each other, might not a little contribute to the alacrity they shewed on this occasion. In effect, the quickness of their progress surprized and delighted Mr. Markham, their present tutor, as well as their former one, that is their Mama, to whom they would run every day in raptures of joy to communicate the contents of their several lessons.

Hitherto we have seen Eugene, Richard, and Cassander, perfectly alike and equal in all things; it is necessary now to shew in what respects they were unlike, and how the particular character and disposition of each, though leading to actions extremely different from what the others would pursue, yet always uniformly concurred in the exertion of that amiable principle, brotherly love.

Eugene, therefore, with much generosity, and something of fire in his composition, was at the same time a little arch, or what is called waggish. His pranks, in general, were the most innocent

nocent in the world, it is true, and he could say
at least that he never meant to hurt: if, however,
it would sometimes happen, which after all was
seldom the case, that any of his little jokes cost
either of his brothers a tear, that tear, it was easy
to be seen, gave Eugene infinitely more pain
than any he himself shed: but the open frank-
ness and ardent good nature with which he would
console his weeping brother, seldom failed to
dry it up in a moment. He would never justify
his own mistakes nor his aukwardness; and thus
he seldom felt the reproaches of his companions,
because they always found him ready to submit
to them candidly, and, whenever it so happened,
to own himself in fault.

Richard, on the other hand, was all simplicity: he had not the least shadow of design in
him; and were it not for the extraordinary ap-
prehension that he shewed in his learning, in
which he outstripped both his brothers, he might
be said not to have a thought of his own. Thus
Richard, though as cheerful as the day, seldom
laughed unless Eugene or Cassander led the joke.
He never proposed a new sort of play, or invented a fresh plaything, but always was ready,
with the greatest good humour, to join in the
one or admire the other, if offered to his atten
tion by either of his brothers. He might even
be said to have no wants or likings of his
own,

own, but as they put him in mind of them. If Eugene ſaid to the maid, " Molly, I want to go to bed;" Richard would add, " ſo do I too." If Caſſander ſaid, " Mama, pray give me a piece " of bread and butter," Richard, if preſent, would commonly join, " Aye, and me too."— And this diſpoſition of Richard was the happieſt in the world, for preſerving the friendſhip of the Three Brothers; ſince, whatever advantage or ſuperiority he might have in his learning, all his amuſements, all the pleaſure that he enjoyed from ſociety, depended wholly on Eugene and Caſſander.

This laſt was neither ſo volatile as his elder brother, nor ſo ſimple as Richard: he had ſomething grave even in his countenance, and though youngeſt of the three, was allowed to be much the moſt prudent; by which means he balanced, as it were, the oppoſite defects of his brothers, and frequently would act as their adviſer and cenſor, by reproving Eugene for his too great vivacity, which led him ſo often into ſcrapes, and Richard for his thoughtleſs abſence and extreme credulity. But though he ſometimes took this freedom, it was always with the greateſt tenderneſs, being accuſtomed from his infancy to treat his elders with reſpect, particularly his brothers. Indeed, a reſpect for their elders and ſuperiors Mrs. Smithſon took early care to inculcate

cate on the minds of all her children. Richard was commanded to yield in every thing to Eugene, and Caſſander to Richard; and all three to behave with proper deference to thoſe who were more advanced in life than themſelves. This injunction had a good effect more ways than one: it prevented any childiſh conteſts for the preference, as each knew and was contented with his own rank, and always waited his proper turn. Beſides, it made them behave with good manners to ſtrangers, let their condition in life be what it will; nor was any one of them ever known to ſpeak or act with petulance even to a beggar.

After remaining a competent time under the inſtruction of Mr. Markham, it was their father's pleaſure that they ſhould all three enter the Univerſity together, and purſue their ſtudies there, in order to qualify themſelves for whatever of the learned profeſſions they might afterwards chuſe. This circumſtance gave them infinite pleaſure. The love that they bore to each other while children, was now ripening into a ſteady, ardent friendſhip, which no time could alter or diminiſh; and they ſaw before them a proſpect of being happy in each other's ſociety during the whole courſe of their lives. But human events are uncertain, and the ſhades of misfortune often intervene unexpectedly to chequer

the

the most equal and placid sunshine of prosperity. Mr. Smithson was still in trade, and therefore liable to accidents and crosses which merchants frequently experience. It happened, in the beginning of the war, that two ships, containing property of his to a very considerable amount, uninsured, were taken by the enemy. The deficiency produced in his capital by this misfortune, joined to several other smaller losses, obliged Mr. Smithson to become a bankrupt; after which, conceiving a distaste to his native place, he determined to take a voyage to the West-Indies, in order to look after an estate in land, which had been bequeathed him as a legacy by some distant relation since the time of his failure. At his departure, not judging it expedient to take his wife along with him, he left her a small sum of ready money, but promised to send over remittances whenever the property, of which he went to take possession, could be turned to any account.

Our Three Brothers were inconsolable at parting with their father; this was the first time in their lives that they might be said to feel the grief of absence from their beloved parents; for while at College they could hardly be called absent from home, as they conversed weekly, nay, almost daily, by letters, either with Mr. or Mrs. Smithson.

Smithson. But their sorrow was considerably increased, when, after two years had elapsed without any tidings from their father, they received a melancholy epistle from Mrs. Smithson, informing them of her utter inability to maintain them any longer at College, and requesting their immediate return, in order to consult how they should dispose of themselves for their future settlement in life.

During the last two years that they had spent at the University, nothing but the strictest œconomy, on the part of the Brothers, as well as that of their indulgent parent, could have enabled them to subsist; yet, notwithstanding the general dissipation of the place, their temperance and frugality did not hinder them from supporting an amiable character, and being highly esteemed by all who knew them. They were remarked for an obliging, affable demeanour, an unexceptionable attention to their College duties, but particularly for the strict intimacy and happy degree of unanimity which they always appeared to maintain. They were, indeed distinguished by the title of *The Three Brothers;* and the wits of the place spoke of them as an exception to that remark of the poet,

> Friendship, like love, is but a name,
> Unless to one you stint the flame.

However,

However, there was a confiderable difference in their difpofitions, which, without the leaft impairing their affection, grew every day more and more confpicuous. Eugene was now ambitious, enterprizing, and changeable: his parts were rather brilliant than folid. Caffander, on the contrary, was fteady in his opinions and refolutions, which he built on the foundeft and moft mature reflection: he appeared more flow in apprehending the difficulties of fcience than his elder brother; but, in return, his memory was more faithful and retentive, and whatever knowledge he once made his own was ever after at his command; for, as Mr. Pope elegantly obferves,

> Where beams of warm imagination play,
> The memory's foft figures melt away.

Richard was a fort of *medium* between thefe oppofites: with fomething of Eugene's vivacity and
the

the steadiness of Cassander, he had an ardent and insatiable thirst of knowledge; in effect, he had recommended himself so powerfully to his superiors, by the extent and splendour of his attainments, that he was, at this very time of Mrs. Smithson's writing for him and his brothers, pointed out to a nobleman, equally respectable for his rank and principles, as a proper person to be private tutor to his Lordship's two sons, who were lately entered at the University.

At their return therefore, upon the summons of their mother, when she laid before them the melancholy state of their affairs, the disappointment of their expectations, and, to crown all, the dreadful apprensions that she entertained of the loss of her husband, either at sea or by the casualties of war, concluding with the tenderest advice to them, to unite their efforts towards the re-establishing of their circumstances by a steady course of industry, in whatever professions they might adopt: upon this occasion it was that the advantages of superior application and a more rapid progress in learning appeared conspicuous. While Eugene and Cassander endeavoured to comfort Mrs. Smithson by the strongest assurances of their future diligence, and the exertion of their industry in some line or other that might afford themselves and her a decent maintenance, Richard had the happiness of being able to make

his

his mother and brothers the immediate tender of a small competency from the salary which his noble patron was to allow him, who only waited for his answer to invest him with the care of his children's education. This prospect was a seasonable relief to Mrs. Smithson from the despondency into which the present gloom of her affairs had thrown her. It is true, the iron hand of want had not as yet begun to pinch her and her children, but the near approach of that unwelcome visitor (without such a resource as Richard now suggested) was sufficient to fill her mind with the most melancholy ideas and dismal presages of adversity and distress.

Now, therefore, at length, by the irresistible decree of necessity, were our Three Brothers obliged to part, and take different walks on the vast theatre of life. Richard, returning to the University, attached himself with so much success to the education of his noble pupils, and to his own improvement, that, besides being able for the present to contribute to the comforts of his mother, and those whom he held most dear next to her, he had the prospect before him of obtaining an ample settlement in the church, through the interest of his munificent patron, whose favour he enjoyed in as full a measure as his numerous good qualities entitled him to it. Eugene having procured recommendations to a

merchant

merchant in London, repaired thither, and, applying himself steadily to business, in the course of four years gave such proofs of his integrity and other good qualifications, that he was taken by the merchant into partnership. Cassander, in the mean time, fearing to become a burthen on the moderate pension that Richard allowed his mother, embraced the offer of a Newcastle trader, who, having formerly been an intimate friend of Mr. Smithson's, agreed to take Cassander a voyage to the East country upon trial. Cassander was still but young, being no more than sixteen at the time of his entering upon a sea life, and after his voyage of trial, he prudently made it his choice, in preference to waiting for the uncertain chance of some more brilliant establishment. In effect, what with the advantage of an excellent education, a patient and humane disposition, and the uncommon character (for a seaman) of being remarkably sober and frugal, he in a very few years so improved himself in the knowledge of trade and navigation, that he was appointed mate of a vessel trading to Russia, the owners of which were so well pleased with his activity and good conduct, that they were determined, notwithstanding his youth, to send him out master of one of their ships the first opportunity that offered.

Thus, for some years after the separation of the

the Three Brothers, fortune seemed to recompence the severe loss that they had felt in the person of their father, concerning whom, all this time, notwithstanding every possible enquiry, not the smallest intelligence had been received. But now, alas! once more, sorrow and adversity came hand in hand to disquiet the feeling hearts of our three youths, by an hour of trial such as they had never yet experienced. The news of their mother's death was the severe prelude to their misfortunes. Richard had scarcely recovered the shock of this, when the death of his patron totally dissipated all the flattering hopes that he had formed of fortune and preferment in the church, in which he had already taken orders. Eugene, and his partner had for some time felt their affairs in a critical condition; but this did not hinder him from exerting his native generosity in the service of an ancient friend. Indeed, the voice of friendship and gratitude always met with a favourable hearing from Eugene, let their summons be ever so pressing and importunate. His old tutor, Mr. Markham, under whom he and his brothers had spent some of the happiest years of their life, was at this time in London. Disabled by sickness and infirmity, advancing fast towards helpless old age, and sorely galled by poverty and the neglect of the world, he was almost

I without

without a friend. In this crisis, chance threw his generous pupil in his way, who amply sup-

plied the place of one to him. Besides furnishing him with the means of supplying his present necessity, Eugene, and by his persuasion his partner, became security for the payment of a very considerable debt, which was on the point of consigning Mr. Markham to a gaol, where he might probably have passed the remainder of his life. But how ill did fortune requite Eugene for this friendly action! Mr. Markham died in less than three months after, when of course the debt devolved upon those who had given security for him. Immediately upon the heels of this misfortune followed another. The affairs of Eugene's partnership growing desperate, they were obliged to declare themselves bankrupt, and this very kindness which he shewed Mr.
Markham

Markham was reckoned among the misfortunes that contributed to his ruin. The shock that Eugene's spirits suffered upon this occasion, as he found himself now unable to fulfil engagements which he looked upon as sacred, drove him from one act of rashness and despair to another, till in the end, reduced to extremity of went, in an obscure country place, he madly and precipitately threw himself among a company of travelling players, and, to crown all, in this unpromising state of life, being barely able to subsist himself, he had the desperate imprudence to marry. It seems he had formed a slight acquaintance with a young lady (the daughter of a clergyman, who was so struck with his figure and accomplishments, that she yielded to his solicitations to be united with him in the ties of clandestine wedlock, thereby utterly forfeiting all her expectations of fortune, together with the friendship of every one of her relations. The consequences of this unadvised step, which brought poverty and her train into Eugene's habitation, in shapes unknown before, he bore with as much fortitude and philosophy as usually falls to the share of five and twenty, that is, with very little, if any at all. Some time before this, Cassander, who had made two or three voyages for his north-country owners, was invited to London by his brother and his partner, to take the command of one of the large ships in which they were principal proprietors. Overjoyed at this invitation, which would give him an opportunity, or rather indeed lay him under the necessity, of being frequently with his brother while on shore, he came to town with all speed, and was just time enough to be witness to the unfortunate failure of Eugene and his associate in trade.

Thus were the Three Brothers plunged into circumstances of the most helpless distress, just at a time when they entertained hopes (apparently well founded) of fixing themselves to their satisfaction for life in their respective professions. Had any one of them been exempt from the pressure of misfortune, the other two would have been sure of partaking with him in the comforts that depend on a competency of wealth. But all three were equally reduced; and the only remnant of happiness, that they could call their own, was the sense of their mutual affection, which still continued unalterable, amidst the most pinching trials of disappointment and calamity. In this situation were the Smithsons, when an incident happened which put that affection to the proof, and brought forth instances of self-denial and generosity that well deserve to be recorded. In the course of Eugene's wanderings as a country player,

player, fortune conducted him to Gravesend, where, as he was exhibiting before an audience, chiefly composed of seafaring people, the same fortune unaccountably led his father to become a spectator of his performance. In order to explain the sudden appearance of Mr. Smithson, it will be necessary to relate what befel him after his departure from England. The reader will remember that this gentleman had set sail for the West Indies, in order to take possession of an estate in one of the islands there; but, having pretty early intelligence that the enemy were masters of the island, and therefore apprehending numberless obstacles to his obtaining clear and quiet possession of the estate; he formed the immediate resolution of getting out, if possible, to the East Indies, where he trusted that, by his general knowledge of trade, he should in a short time be able to retrieve his shattered circumstances, and return to his native country with a fortune sufficient to render the remaining years of his life easy and comfortable. At the same time he took another resolution (the source of infinite grief and disquiet to his family), which was, never to inform them of the place of his retirement until he had gained wealth sufficient to release them from the state of indigence and obscurity into which, he was persuaded, his absence must have plunged them.

This object he amply accomplished in ten years, during all which time his family considered him as dead; and at the end of that period he was now returning to share his riches with those whom he held most dear; when the first sight that saluted his eyes after he went on shore was his unfortunate son figuring in the humble profession of a stroller. It is impossible to express the rage, sorrow, and disappointment, which at once took possession of Mr. Smithson's breast, when he was at length convinced that his eyes and ears did not deceive him. He suddenly left the theatre, or rather barn, before the play was half over, and taking no farther notice of his son than to leave a note directed for him, and filled with the bitterest reproaches, he hurried on board the ship. Upon his arrival in London, finding his anxious wishes and all the projects of his affection disconcerted by his eldest son's imprudence; his next care was to make inquiry about Richard and Cassander; for his wife's death he had been informed of by mere accident a short time before he left India. Richard he soon found out, who, upon the first summons, flew to embrace his long lost parent, Mr. Smithson, after briefly relating to him the circumstances of his voyage to and success in the East Indies, began bitterly to lament his misfortune in having a son so abandoned to modesty

and

and difcretion, as he ftyled the unfortunate Eugene. He added, that the bulk of the fortune which he had realized abroad, he intended now to divide between his two younger fons, the elder having proved himfelf fo unworthy of his favour: that he did not mean to keep them in expectation until his death, but would put each of them in immediate poffeffion of an ample fortune; referving for himfelf what he was determined fhould be fufficient for his neceffities during the remainder of his life. He concluded with infifting, that whatever he meant thus to difpofe in favour of his younger fons, he would take care to fee fettled, in fuch a manner, that neither Eugene nor his pofterity fhould ever inherit a penny of it.

Richard modeftly thanked his father for the affectionate care that he teftified for his intereft, but tenderly intreated him not to form too precipitate a refolution to the prejudice of his eldeft born. He ufed many arguments to excufe, or at leaft to palliate Eugene's indifcretion; reprefented the forrowful effects that a continuance of his father's refentment might have upon a mind fo exquifitely feeling as his; and ended with thefe words: "As to what regards my "own perfonal advantage, I affure you, Sir, I "feel myfelf naturally very indifferent; and "were I not fo by nature, the profeffion that I
" have

"have embraced, the precepts of which I have
"with my whole heart confented to obey, that
"profeffion commands me to fix my thoughts
"and expectations upon matters of a far dif-
"ferent nature. Befides, had I the moft worldly
"regard for my own intereft, the affection that
"I have ever borne, and ftill bear to my bro-
"ther Eugene, would ftand as a bar to my ac-
"cepting any fortune to which he had the moft
"diftant claim. I am not without hopes, my
"dear father, that when your prefent anger
"fubfides, you will once more look upon him
"with the tendernefs of a parent, in which cafe
"you will, I truft, applaud the principle that
"induces me to decline your liberal offer."
Mr. Smithfon, with aftonifhment in his countenance, afked his fon if he was ferious in refufing
fo handfome a fortune; and finding him fixed in
the determination that he had before expreffed,
he rofe up with evident marks of vexation and
difappointment; and cafting fome uncharitable
reflections on the deftiny which, he faid, purfued
him through life, baffling and fruftrating the moft
favourite and even laudable wifhes of his heart,
he added in a tone of voice, fomewhat foftened,
"Little did I expect, when I fent for you, to
"find you an abettor of that profligacy which
"has alienated my heart from your elder bro-
"ther. I fondly thought that my children
"would

"would pay such deference to my authority as even to adopt my prejudices; but since you have determined to think for yourself, be your own master. Thank Heaven, I have yet one son left." Richard endeavoured in the most respectful manner, to represent the motives of his conduct, but perceiving that whatever he said only tended to irritate his father, and that it was impossible, for the present, to obtain a calm hearing, he reluctantly withdrew, leaving his father in a situation not to be envied by a parent.

Nothing could arrive more opportunely to relieve the depression of Mr. Smithson's spirits, than the news that he heard next morning; which was, that a ship, in which Caffander had gone out in the capacity of a mate, after the failure of Eugene, was returned from her voyage in the river. His resentment was now not only pointed at Eugene for his indiscretion, but at Richard for his too scrupulous, uncomplying principles. He was therefore determined to bestow his whole fortune upon Caffander. But what language can express the amazement of Mr. Smithson, when, upon his proposing to do so, the generous seaman, without the least hesitation or preamble, flatly refused to accept a penny of it! He thought, however, that respect to his father required him to give the reasons on which he grounded his refusal. He did so; and
with

with arguments nearly the same as those used by his brother Richard, he endeavoured to convince his father that passion had a much greater share than mature deliberation in the sentence which he was going to pass upon his eldest son: "We are all liable to go astray," said Cassander: " happy is he who has the fewest faults. If we do not forgive those of a son, or a brother, Heaven help us when our own come to be judged! As for me, I have lived contented with a little, and am not unacquainted with hardship and distress. God forbid, therefore, that I should grasp at my brother's birth-right. —But I declare, were Eugene no brother of mine, knowing as I do his generous nature and the warmth of his honest heart, I would go before the mast all my life long, sooner than accept, to his prejudice, a property which nature and reason so clearly adjudge to him."

There was something so ingenuous in this address of Cassander's, something that spoke so feelingly to his father's breast, that, in spite of a short conflict which resentment endeavoured to excite there, he found himself constrained to yield the point, and while he wiped away a tear, the offspring of returning tenderness and affection, he took his son by the hand: " Cas-
" sander,"

"fander," faid he, fmiling, "thou haft! con-
"quered. Surely there muft be fomething of
"extraordinary merit in Eugene, fince he has
"found two fo refolute advocates in his favour
"as you and your brother Richard.—Well, I
"forgive all the paft—it fhall be buried in ob-
"livion.—Convince me, as I doubt not you
"will, that my eldeft fon poffeffes qualities
"worthy to excite fuch fentiments as you have
"both expreffed in his favour, and I fhall be
"happy indeed."

It is needlefs to add, that the joy produced by this favourable change in Mr. Smithfon's feelings was foon diffufed to the breafts of his two difconfolate fons. Eugene, upon the receipt of his father's note, had hurried up to town from Gravefend, like one diftracted, and was now at Richard's lodgings, indulging the moft paffionate effufions of grief and defpair; while Richard, depreffed with a load of forrows, fat moping in filence, without a word of comfort to offer to his brother. They hardly perceived Caffander enter the room; but when he met their eyes, they ftarted as at the fight of an angel. Something prophetic whifpered comfort to their minds even before he fpoke. But how full was the meafure of their joy when he announced to them his father's invitation to repair immediately to his

pre-

presence! The sequel is easy to be imagined: all was reconciled: the past was forgotten, and the future opened a prospect of happiness before them more smiling than they had ever enjoyed before.

Thus the Brothers, by the efforts of their mutual affection, increased the happiness that prosperity afforded them, sustained each other, under the pressure of misfortune, and, by persevering in unalterable friendship to each other, at length ensured both their own happiness and that of their dearest and first friend on earth—their Father.

COURAGE INSPIRED BY FRIENDSHIP.

TWO sailors, a Frenchman named Robert, and a native of Spain, called Antonio, were slaves to the same master at Algiers.
Friend-

Friendship is the only consolation of persons in distress. Antonio and Robert happily enjoyed this consolation—they communicated to each other their mutual griefs; they conversed perpetually about their families, their countries, and of the exquisite delight which the recovery of their liberty, should it ever be granted to their wishes, would afford them. Their conferences always ended in a flood of affectionate tears, and this expansion of their hearts enabled them both to support the hard labour, which was their daily lot, with uncommon fortitude.

The task appointed them was the construction of a road on the top of a cliff which overhung the sea. One morning the Spaniard, resting for a moment from his toil, and casting an anxious look on the sea, "My friend," said he, "all "my vows, all my hopes, are directed towards "the opposite bounds of that vast liquid plain; "why can I not, in company with the partner "of my woes, attain those happy shores? My "wife, my children, are ever before my eyes, "eagerly longing for my arrival, or bitterly la- "menting my supposed death." Antonio perpetually indulged himself in these gloomy reflections, and every day that he was summoned to his work on the cliff, he turned his eyes to the ocean, and regretted the fatal expanse which separated him from his friends and his country.

It

It chanced that one day a Christian ship appeared at anchor not very distant from the shore. "There, friend," cried the Spaniard, do you "see that vessel? She brings us life and liberty. "Though she will not touch here, (for every "one avoids these barbarous coasts,) yet to-"morrow if you chuse it, Robert, our woes "shall end, and we will be free! Yes, to-"morrow that ship will pass within a league of "the shore, and we will plunge into the sea "from this rock, or perish in the attempt; for "even death is preferable to this cruel slavery." "If you can save yourself," replied Robert, "I "shall support my unhappy lot with greater re-"signation. You know Antonio, how dear you "are to me; my friendship for you will only "terminate with my life. I have only one "favour to ask of you; endeavour to find out "my father—If grief for my loss, and old age, "have not already destroyed him, tell him"— "What do you mean?" answered Antonio; "I seek your father!—And do you think I "could live happily a single moment with the "idea of having left you in chains?" "But I "cannot swim," cried Robert; "and you "know"—"I know that I have the strongest "friendship for you," replied the Spaniard, embracing him, and shedding tears of affection: "friendship will give me redoubled strength:
"you

"you shall hold up my belt, and we will both save ourselves." In vain did Robert represent the danger there would be of his perishing himself, and dragging his preserver down with him to destruction; nothing could overcome the resolution of Antonio. "We will both escape, or both perish together," he cried. "But we draw the attention of our savage keepers; even some of our companions would be base enough to betray us—Farewel, I hear the bell that calls us from our work; we must separate; farewel till to-morrow!"

They now returned to their dungeon.—Antonio was wrapped up in the idea of his project: he fancied he had already passed the Mediterranean, and was in the arms of his friends, his wife, and his children. But Robert formed to himself a very different picture: he saw his friend falling a victim to his own generosity, and dragged by him to the bottom of the sea, and perishing by that means, when, if he had only consulted his own safety, he might have preserved himself, and been restored to the bosom of his family, who most probably were continually lamenting his loss. "No," said the unfortunate Frenchman to himself, "I will not give way to the solicitations of Antonio; I will not repay so generous a friendship by being the cause of his death. He will be free.

"My

"My unhappy father will at least learn that I
"am alive, and that my affection for him is
"unabated. Alas! I could wish to be the sup-
"port and consolation of his age. He wanted
"my assistance—perhaps he is now perishing in
"poverty, and wishing to see and embrace his
"son. However, if Antonio is happy, I shall
"die with less regret."

The slaves were not taken from their prison the next morning at the usual hour. The Spaniard was all impatience, while Robert was in doubt whether he should rejoice or grieve at the disappointment. At length they were called to their labour, but they could not speak to each other, for their master went with them. Antonio could only look at Robert and sigh. Sometimes he cast his eyes towards the sea, and could hardly suppress his emotions. At length night arrives, and they find themselves alone. "Let us seize this opportunity," cries the Spaniard, "Come!" "No," replies the other:
"my friend I never will consent to endanger
"your life: Farewel, Antonio! I embrace
"you for the last time. Save yourself, I con-
"jure you; you have no time to lose. Re-
"member our friendship. I only request you
"to remember your promise in regard to my fa-
"ther. He must be very old, and much in dis-
"tress; go and console him. If he should want
"assist-

" affiftance, I am fure, my friend——" At thefe words the voice of Robert failed—he fhed a torrent of tears—his bofom was torn with anguifh. " You weep, Robert," fays Antonio : "it is not " tears, but courage, that we now want: refift " no longer; a moment's delay may ruin us; " we may never have the opportunity again; " either deliver yourfelf to my direction, or I " will dafh my head againft thofe rocks."

The Frenchman threw himfelf at the feet of the generous Spaniard: he ftill reprefented the hazard of the attempt, and pointed out the inevitable danger that muft attend his refolution of endeavouring to preferve him. Antonio made no reply, but catching him in his arms, he ran to the edge of the precipice, and plunged with him into the fea. At firft they both funk; but, rifing to the furface, Antonio exerted all his force, and fwimming himfelf, kept Robert alfo above the water, who feemed to refufe his affiftance, and to fear left he fhould involve him in his own deftruction.

The people in the fhip were ftruck with an object which they could not well diftinguifh. They thought it was fome fea-monfter that approached the veffel. Their curiofity was now called another way; they faw a boat leave the fhore, and haftily purfue what feemed to them a monftrous fea animal. Thefe were the foldiers
who

who guarded the flaves, and who were anxious to overtake Antonio and Robert. The laſt faw them approach, and, caſting his eyes on his friend, and perceiving that he grew weak, he made an effort, and got looſe from Antonio, ſaying to him at the ſame time, "We are purſued. "Save yourſelf, and let me periſh; I only retard "your courſe." He had hardly finiſhed theſe words when he ſunk. A new tranſport of friendſhip animates the Spaniard; he darts towards the Frenchman, and ſeizing him as he is juſt ready to expire, they both diſappeared.

The boat, uncertain which way to purſue, ſtopped, while another was ſent from the veſſel to diſcover what the object was which they had ſeen. The waves began to grow rough; at laſt they diſcovered two men, the one ſupporting the other, and trying to reach the veſſel. They rowed to them as faſt as poſſible, and came up with them juſt as Antonio's ſtrength began to fail. They took them both on board. Antonio cried out feebly, "Aſſiſt my friend—I die;"—and his countenance ſeemed convulſed with the agonies of death. Robert, who was in a ſwoon, recovering at the inſtant, and ſeeing Antonio, without any ſign of life, extended by his ſide, was almoſt diſtracted; he threw himſelf on the body of his friend. "Antonio!" he cried, "my dear An-
"tonio, my friend, my deliverer, have I been
"your

" your murderer? Alas! you cannot hear me.—
" Is this your recompence for having saved my
" life? But what is life? Who can support it
" after the lofs of such a friend?"

Saying this, he started up in the boat, and, seizing a sword, would have plunged it into his bosom, if he had not been disarmed; but, in the midst of his lamentations and distraction, Providence, apparently to reward an affection so sincere, interposed in his favour—Antonio breathed a sigh. Robert flew to the assistance of his friend, who, lifting up his languid eyes, tried to find the Frenchman, and, as soon as he perceived him, cried out with a transport beyond his strength, " I have saved my friend!"

They were both conveyed on board the vessel. Their exemplary friendship diffused a respect for them among the whole crew. And, such is the effect of virtue even on the roughest minds, every one contended with his fellows in shewing them attention. Robert arriving in France flew to his father, who was ready to die with excess of joy at seeing him, and was appointed to a genteel office under the Government. But the Spaniard, who was likewise offered a very advantageous post, for one in his situation of life, chose rather to return to his wife and family. But absence did not diminish his friendship; he continued still to correspond with Robert, and

their

their letters, which are masterpieces of simplicity and affection, do honour to the sentiment which was capable of producing so heroic an action.

THE

THE DIVERTING HISTORY OF
JOHN GILPIN;

Shewing how he went farther than he intended, and came safe Home again.

JOHN Gilpin was a citizen
 Of credit and renown;
A train-band captain eke was he
 Of famous London town.

John Gilpin's spouse said to her dear—
 " Though wedded we have been
" These twice ten tedious years, yet we
 " No holiday have seen.

" To-morrow is our wedding day,
 " And we will then repair,
" Unto the Bell at Edmonton,
 " All in a chaise and pair.

" My sister and my sister's child,
 " Myself and children three,
" Will fill the chaise; so you must ride
 " On horseback after we."

He soon replied—" I do admire
 " Of womankind but one,
" And you are she, my dearest dear,
 " Therefore it shall be done.

" I am a linen-draper bold,
 " As all the world doth know,
And my good friend the callender,
 " Will lend his horse to go."

Quoth

Quoth Mrs. Gilpin—" That's well said;
  " And, for that wine is dear,
" We will be furnish'd with our own,
  " Which is both bright and clear."

John Gilpin kiss'd his loving wife:
  O'erjoy'd was he to find,
That, though on pleasure she was bent,
  She had a frugal mind.

The morning came, the chaise was brought,
  But yet was not allow'd
To drive up to the door, lest all
  Should say that she proud.

So three doors off the chaise was staid,
  Where they did all get in,
Six precious souls' and all agog
  To dash through thick and thin.

Smack went the whip, round went the wheels,
  Were never folks so glad;
The stones did rattle underneath,
  As if Cheapside were mad.

John Gilpin at his horse's side,
  Seiz'd fast the flowing mane,
And up he got, in haste to ride,
  But soon came down again.

For saddle-tree scarce reach'd had he,
  His journey to begin,
When, turning round his head, he saw
  Three customers come in.

So down he came; for loſs of time,
   Although it griev'd him ſore,
Yet loſs of pence, full well he knew,
   Would trouble him much more.

'Twas long before the cuſtomers
   Were ſuited to their mind,
When Betty, ſcreaming, came down ſtairs,
   " The wine is left behind !"

" Good lack !" quoth he—" yet bring it me,
   " My leathern belt likewiſe,
" In which I bear my truſty ſword
   " When I do exerciſe."

Now Mrs. Gilpin—careful ſoul—
   Had two ſtone bottles found,
To hold the liquor that ſhe lov'd,
   And keep it ſafe and ſound.

Each bottle had a curling ear,
   Through which the belt he drew;
And hung a bottle on each ſide,
   To make his balance true.

Then over all, that he might be
   Equipp'd from top to toe,
His long red cloak, well bruſhed and neat,
   He manfully did throw.

Now ſee him mounted once again
   Upon his nimble ſteed,
Full ſlowly pacing o'er the ſtones,
   With caution and good heed.

                            But

But finding foon a fmoother road
  Beneath his well-fhod feet,
The fnorting beaft began to trot,
  Which gall'd him in his feat,

So, "Fair and foftly," John he cried,
  But John he cried in vain;
That trot became a gallop foon,
  In fpite of kirb and rein.

So ftooping down, as needs he muft
  Who cannot fit upright,
He grafp'd the mane with both his hands,
  And eke with all his might.

His horfe, who never in that fort
  Had handled been before,
What thing upon his back had got
  Did wonder more and more.

Away went Gilpin, neck or nought,
  Away went hat and wig;
He little dreamt when he fet out,
  Of running fuch a rig.

The wind did blow, the cloak did fly,
  Like ftreamer long and gay,
Till loop and button failing both,
  At laft it flew away.

Then might all people well difcern
  The bottles he had flung;
A bottle fwinging at each fide,
  As hath been faid or fung.

The

The dogs did bark, the children scream'd,
  Up flew the windows all;
And ev'ry soul cried out, " Well done!"
  As loud as he could bawl.

Away went Gilpin—who but he!
  His fame soon spread around—
" He carries weight!—he rides a race!—
  " 'Tis for a thousand pound!

And still, as fast as he drew near,
  'Twas wonderful to view,
How, in a trice, the turnpike-men
  Their gates wide open threw.

And now as he went bowing down
  His reeking head full low,
The bottles twain behind his back,
  Were shattered at a blow.

Down ran the wine into the road,
  Most piteous to be seen,
Which made his horse's flanks to smoke
  As they had basted been.

But still he seem'd to carry weight,
  With leather girdle brac'd;
For all might see the bottle-necks
  Still dangling at his waist.

Thus all through merry Islington,
  These gambols he did play,
And till he came unto the Wash
  Of Edmonton so gay;

And there he threw the Wash about
   On both sides of the way,
Just like unto a trundling-mop,
   Or a wild goose at play.

At Edmonton his loving wife
   From the balcony spied
Her tender husband, wond'ring much
   To see how he did ride.

" Stop, stop, John Gilpin ; here's the house !"
   They all at once did cry ;
" The dinner waits, and we are tir'd !"—
   Said Gilpin—" So am I."

But yet his horse was not a whit
   Inclin'd to tarry there ;
For why ?—his owner had a house
   Full ten miles off, at Ware.

So like an arrow swift he flew,
   Shot by an archer strong ;
So did he fly—which brings me to
   The middle of my song.

Away went Gilpin out of breath,
   And sore against his will,
Till at his friend the callender's
   His horse at last stood still.

The callender, amaz'd to see
   His neighbour in such trim,
Laid down his pipe, flew to the gate
   And thus accosted him—

                        " What

" What news! what news! your tidings tell,
 " Tell me you muſt and ſhall—
" Say, why bare headed you are come,
 Or why you come at all?"

Now Gilpin had a pleaſant wit,
 And lov'd a timely joke;
And thus unto the callender
 In merry guiſe he ſpoke—

" I came becauſe your horſe would come;
 " And, if I well forebode,
" My hat and wig will ſoon be here;
 They are upon the road."

The callender right glad to find
 His friend in merry pin,
Return'd him not a ſingle word,
 But to the houſe went in.

Whence ſtraight he came with hat and wig,
 A wig that flow'd behind,
A hat not much the worſe for wear,
 Each comely in its kind.

He held them up, and, in his turn,
 Thus ſhew'd his ready wit—
" My head is twice as big as yours,
 " They, therefore, needs muſt fit.

" But let me ſcrape the dirt away
 " That hangs upon your face;
" And ſtop and eat—for well you may
 Be in a hungry caſe!

Said John—" It is my wedding day,
   " And all the world would ſtare,
" If wife ſhould dine at Edmonton,
   And I ſhould dine at Ware."

So turning to his horſe, he ſaid
   " I am in haſte to dine;
" 'Twas for your pleaſure you came here—
   You ſhall go back for mine."

Ah! luckleſs ſpeech and bootleſs boaſt,
   For which he paid full dear;
For, while he ſpake, a braying aſs
   Did ſing moſt loud and clear;

Whereat his horſe did ſnort, as he
   Had heard a lion roar,
And gallopp'd off with all his might,
   As he had done before.

Away went Gilpin—and away
   Went Gilpin's hat and wig;
He loſt them ſooner than at firſt,
   For why?—they were too big.

Now Mrs. Gilpin, when ſhe ſaw
   Her huſband poſting down
Into the country far away,
   She pull'd out half-a-crown;

And thus unto the youth ſhe ſaid
   That drove them to the Bell,
" This ſhall be yours, when you bring back
   " My huſband ſafe and well."

The youth did ride, and foon did meet
    John coming back again,
Whom in a trice he tried to ftop,
    By catching at his rein;

But not performing what he meant,
    And gladly would have done,
The frighted fteed he frighted more,
    And made him fafter run.

Away went Gilpin—and away
    Went poft-boy at his heels,
The poft-boy's horfe right glad to mifs
    The lumb'ring of the wheels.

Six gentlemen upon the road,
    Thus feeing Gilpin fly,
With poft-boy fcamp'ring in the rear,
    They rais'd the hue-and-cry.

" Stop thief!—ftop thief!—a highwayman!"
    Not one of them was mute;
And all and each that pafs'd that way
    Did join in the purfuit.

And now the turnpike gates again
    Flew open in fhort fpace,
The toll-men thinking, as before,
    That Gilpin rode a race.

And fo he did, and won it too;
    For he got firft to town,
Nor ftopp'd till where he had got up
    He did again get down.

Now let us sing—" Long live the King;
"And Gilpin, long live he;
"And when he next doth ride abroad,
"May I be there to see!"

GRAY's ELEGY.

Written in a Country Church-Yard.

THE curfew tolls the knell of parting day,
    The lowing herd winds flowly o'er the lee,
The plowman homeward plods his wearied way,
    And leaves the world to darknefs and to me.

Now fades the glimmering landfkip on the fight,
    And all the air a folemn ftillnefs holds;
Save where the beetle wheels his droning flight,
    Or drowfy tinkling lulls the diftant folds:

Save that from yonder ivy-mantled tow'r,
    The moping owl does to the moon complain
Of fuch as, wand'ring near the fecret bow'r,
    Moleft her ancient—folitary reign.

Beneath thefe rugged elms—that yew-tree's fhade,
    Where heaves the turf in a many a mould'ring heap,
Each in his narrow cell for ever laid,
    The rude forefathers of the hamlet fleep.

The breezy call of incenfe-breathing morn,
    The fwallow twitt'ring from her ftraw-built fhed,
The cock's fhrill clarion, or the echoing horn,
    No more fhall rouze them from their lowly bed.

For them no more the blazing hearth shall burn,
    Or busy housewife ply her evening care,
No children run to lisp their sire's return,
    Or climb his knees the envy'd kiss to share.

Oft did the harvest to the sickle yield,
    Their harrow oft the stubborn glebe had broke,
How jocund did they drive their team a-field!
    How bow'd the woods beneath their sturdy stroke!

Let not ambition mock their useful toil,
    Their homely joys and destiny obscure,
Nor grandeur here, with a disdainful smile,
    The short and simple annals of the poor.

The boast of heraldry, the pomp of pow'r,
    All that beauty—all that wealth e'er gave,
Await alike th' inevitable hour;
    The paths to glory lead but to the grave.

Nor you, ye proud, impute to those the fault,
    If mem'ry o'er their tomb no trophies raise,
Where thro' the long-drawn isle and fretted vault,
    The pealing anthem swells the note of praise.

Can story'd urn, or animated bust,
    Back to its mansion call the fleeting breath?
Can honour's voice provoke the silent dust,
    Or flatt'ry sooth the dull cold ear of death?

Perhaps in this neglected spot is laid
    Some heart once pregnant with celestial fire:
Hands that the reins of empire might have sway'd,
    Or wake to ecstacy the living lyre.

But knowledge to their eyes her ample page,
    Rich with the spoils of time, did ne'er unroll;
Chill penury repress'd their noble rage,
    And froze the genial current of the soul.

Full many a gem of purest ray serene
    The dark unfathom'd caves of ocean bear;
Full many a flower is born to blush unseen,
    And waste its sweetness on the desart air.

Some village *Hampden*, that, with dauntless breast,
    The little tyrant of his fields withstood;
Some mute, inglorious *Milton* here may rest;
    Some *Cromwell*, guiltless of his country's blood.

Th' applause of list'ning senates to command,
    The threats of pain and ruin to despise,
To scatter plenty o'er a smiling land,
    And read their hist'ry in a nation's eyes.

Their lot forbade: not circumscrib'd alone
    Their growing virtues, but their crimes confin'd:
Forbade to wade through slaughter to a throne,
    And shut the gates of mercy on mankind.

The struggling pangs of conscious truth to hide,
    To quench the blushes of ingenuous shame,
Or heap the shrine of luxury and pride
    With incense kindled at the Muse's flame.

Far from the madding crowd's ignoble strife,
    Their sober wishes never learn'd to stray:
Along the cool sequester'd vale of life,
    They kept the noiseless tenor of their way.

Yet e'en these bones from insult to protect
  Some frail memorial still erected nigh,
With uncouth rhymes and shapeless sculpture deck'd,
  Implores the passing tribute of a sigh.

Their name, their years, spelt by th' unletter'd Muse,
  The place of fame and elegy supply,
And many a holy text around she strews,
  To teach the rustic moralist to die.

For who, to dumb forgetfulness a prey,
  This pleasing anxious being e'er resign'd,
Left the warm precincts of the cheerful day,
  Nor cast one longing, ling'ring look behind!

On some fond breast the parting soul relies,
  Some pious drop the closing eye requires;
Ev'n from the tomb the voice of nature cries,
  Ev'n in our ashes live their wonted fires.

For thee, who, mindful of the unhonour'd dead,
  Dost in these lines their artless tale relate,
If chance by lonely contemplation led,
  Some kindred spirit shall inquire thy fate:

Haply some hoary-headed swain may say,
  " Oft have we seen him at the peep of dawn
" Brushing with hasty steps the dews away,
  " To meet the sun upon the upland lawn.

" There at the foot of yonder nodding beech,
  " That wreaths its old fantastic roots so high,
" His listless length at noon-tide would he stretch,
  " And pore upon the brook that bubbles by.

" Hard by yon wood, now fmilling as in fcorn,
   " Mutt'ring his wayward fancies, he would rove ;
" Now drooping, woeful wan, like one forlorn,
   " Or craz'd with care, or crofs'd in hopelefs love.

" One morn I mifs'd him on the cuftom'd hill,
   " Along the heath, and near his fav'rite tree ;
" Another came, nor yet befide the rill,
   " Nor up the lawn, nor at the wood was he:

" The next, with dirges due, in fad array,
   " Slow through the church-way path we faw him
      borne ;
" Approach and read (for thou canft read) the lay
   " Grav'd on the ftone beneath yon aged thorn.

" There fcatter'd oft, the earlieft of the year,
   " By hands unfeen are fhowers of violets found ;
" The red-breaft loves to build and warble there,
   " And little footfteps lightly print the ground."

THE EPITAPH.

HERE refts his head upon the lap of earth,
   A youth to fortune and to fame unknown:
Fair fcience frown'd not on his humble birth,
   And melancholy mark'd him for her own.

Large was his bounty, and his foul fincere ;
   Heav'n did a recompence as largely fend ;
He gave to mis'ry (all he had) a tear ;
   He gain'd from Heav'n ('twas all he wifh'd) a
      friend.

No farther seek his merits to disclose,
   Or draw his frailties from their dread abode,
(There they alike in trembling hope repose)
   The bosom of his Father and his God.

THE UNIVERSAL PRAYER.

FATHER of all! in ev'ry age,
   In ev'ry clime ador'd,
By saint, by savage, and by sage,
   Jehovah, *Jove*, or *Lord*.

Thou Great First Cause, least understood,
   Who all my sense confin'd
To know but this, that thou art good,
   And that myself am blind.

Yet gave me in this dark estate
   To see the good from from ill;
And binding nature fast in fate,
   Left free the human will.

What conscience dictates to be done,
   Or warns me not to do,
This, teach me more than hell to shun,
   That, more than heav'n pursue.

What blessings thy free bounty gives,
   Let me not cast away;
For God is paid when man receives,
   T' enjoy is to obey.

Yet not to earth's contracted span
    Thy goodness let me bound,
Or think thee Lord alone of man,
    When thousand worlds are round.

Let not this weak unknowing hand
    Presume thy bolts to throw,
Or deal damnation round the land,
    On each I judge thy foe.

If I am right, thy grace impart
    Still in the right to stay!
If I am wrong, O teach my heart
    To find the better way.

Save me alike from foolish pride,
    Or impious discontent,
At aught thy wisdom has deny'd,
    Or aught thy goodness lent.

Teach me to feel another's woe,
    To hide the fault I see;
That mercy I to others shew,
    That mercy shew to me.

Mean tho' I am, not wholly so,
    Since quicken'd by thy breath;
O lead me wheresoe'er I go,
    Thro' this day's life or death.

This day be bread and peace my lot;
    All else beneath the sun
Thou know'st if best bestow'd, or not,
    And let thy will be done.

To thee whofe temple is all fpace,
  Whofe altar, earth, fea, fkies,
One chorus let all beings raife!
  All Nature's incenfe rife!

THE DUEL; OR, THE MAN OF TRUE COURAGE.

MELCOUR loft his parents at an age when he could not be fenfible of the greatnefs of his misfortune. One of his uncles took him home, brought him up with his own fon, and paid the utmoft attention to his education. Florival and Melcour, already united by the ties of kindred, were foon more fo by thofe of friendfhip, which, from their living conftantly together, grew ftronger every day. They were both defigned for the army. When they were of a proper age, they got commiffions in the fame regiment. Florival always hated application, and the diffipation that naturally attends a military life ftill inclined him lefs to it. As for Melcour, he had not only a very good natural genius, but ftrong inclination to cultivate it. His ftudies had been properly directed; and a generous and humane difpofition, joined with a habit of thinking ferioufly, led him to condemn the criminal practice of fighting duels on trivial occafions, a cuftom too prevalent in the army.

Different

Different purfuits leffened, by degrees, the friendfhip of the two young men. Florival was blinded by the love of pleafure, he ran into all forts of extravagance, and became involved in debt. Melcour lamented his folly, affifted him with his purfe, and endeavoured to fave him from the ruin into which he was going to plunge. He reprefented to him how much his conduct degraded him in the eyes of fenfible people. " Even thofe," faid he to him, " who now ap-
" plaud your extravagance, will be the firft to
" upbraid you when they fee you in diftrefs.
" They call themfelves your beft friends, and
" you believe them: they have eftranged you
" from me. They have painted me to you in
" the moft unfavourable colours, and if they
" have not entirely extinguifhed the friendfhip
" that fubfifted between us, at leaft they have
" greatly weakened it. The wretches well knew
" my fincere affection for you; they are inform-
" ed of the pains I have taken to difcover to you
" their perfidious defigns, and they wifh to pu-
" nifh me for them. O, my friend, if they fhould
" fucceed in robbing me of your efteem, their
" triumph will be too complete! But, my dear
" Florival, I do not fpeak on my own account
" only. I conjure you, by every fentiment of
" virtue that united our infancy, not to plunge
" a dagger in the heart of the beft of fathers. If
" he

" he were to know the excesses you run into, he
" would die with sorrow.

These remonstrances touched the heart of Florival. He promised to amend; but his perfidious friends represented vice to him in so amiable a form, that he was unable to resist. Melcour being informed, that, after having lost a great sum of money at play, he was gone to dissipate his sorrow by infamous debauchery, immediately went to him, and urged to him, with some vehemence, the duties of his situation, and the promises he had made to fulfil them.

Florival was no longer master of himself; he fell into a most violent rage against his cousin; he even drew his sword on him; and on Melcour's refusing to fight him, he abused him in the grossest terms, and was almost tempted to strike him. His cousin still kept his temper; unworthy as Florival appeared of his affection, he yet only regarded him as a friend and relation.

Overcome by this steadiness, he at length recovered his temper. He was ashamed of his behaviour, and begged pardon of Melcour for his violence, which was immediately granted by the generous youth, and an immediate and perfect reconciliation took place.

An officer belonging to another regiment happened to be present during the affair; he had been witness to the provocation given by Florival,

val, and he imputed the coolness of his cousin to want of courage. He did not fail to make many sarcastic remarks on it, and they came at length to the ears of some of Melcour's friends. The least suspicion is deemed injurious to the honour of a soldier. After many enquiries, it was discovered whose conduct had given rise to the scandal. They were told the honour of the corps was wounded through them, and it was their duty to vindicate it. The means were evident. If the report was true, they must fight each other; if false, they must punish the author of it. Melcour was truly miserable. His principles disapproved of duelling in any instance; and in this, if he obeyed the injunctions of his corps, he was reduced to the terrible necessity of plunging his sword into the bosom of his relation and friend. But, in vain did he represent his feelings to his brother officers, they would hear of nothing but the choice of weapons, time, and place. His sorrow was unutterable; he retired to his apartment. Florival, who went to look for him, found him leaning on a table, hiding his face with his hands, his eyes streaming with tears, and his continual sighs, only interrupted by the frequent repetition of the name of Florival. At such a sight he was not able to contain himself; he threw himself at the feet of his friend. His appearance recalled

recalled to Melcour all the horror of his situation—" What! in a moment I am called upon "to pierce your heart, and do you come to seek "me?—O Florival!" said he, his voice almost choaked with tears, "should my arm deprive "you of life, I would not survive you. What "should I say to your father? Did he take so "much care of my infancy, to see me stained "with the blood of his son? O, wretched old "man, whatever may be the event of this hor-"rid duel, it will be an eternal source of an-"guish for you!"

At this instant some of the officers forced open the door; they came to tell Melcour he could not delay the combat any longer without giving room to call his courage in question.— What a terrible situation!—At this instant the two friends were embracing each other—they were unable to return any answer.

Florival was the first who broke this mournful silence. In him the mistaken principles of honour at present prevailed over those of friendship. He got up, and extended his arm to assist Melcour, without daring to look at him. He arose, and walked about the room in the greatest agitation; he fancied he saw his relation and friend murdered by his hands, and his distracted uncle demanding vengeance for the blood of his son. At length, recovering himself, he turned
to

to the officers, and said to them in a firm and resolute tone of voice: "I will no longer hesi-"tate to act that part which is pointed out to "me by the voice of religion, of reason, and of "humanity, be the consequence what it may. "My determination is fixed. Go, and inform "those who sent you, that Melcour prefers an "*imaginary* dishonour to a *real* crime, and that "no consideration upon earth shall tempt him "to point his sword against the bosom of his "friend." This answer determined his fate. His brother officers informed him, with the sincerest regret, that, as he had refused to fight, it was impossible for them to roll with him, and that he must quit the regiment. Who can describe the feelings of Florival, when he heard this sentence? It was *he* who had brought Melcour into this terrible situation. The disgrace of his cousin was owing to *his* follies. These thoughts almost drove him to distraction. His friends were alarmed for the consequence, and removed him by force from the mournful scene.

Melcour, left to himself, soon determined what steps to take. He was determined not to return home, to be there exposed to a disgrace he was conscious of not deserving. He resolved to endeavour to improve the talents which Nature had endowed him with by travelling, till time should either obliterate the memory of this

this unfortunate adventure, or fhew it in its true light. That very evening he made the proper preparations for his journey, and wrote a letter to his coufin, acquainting him with his intended expedition. " Inform my uncle," he added, " of
" all that has happened; let him know that they
" wanted to compel me to become your murderer.
" He will fhudder at the thought. Though thefe
" barbarians, guided only by a falfe fenfe of ho-
" nour, think me unworthy to ferve my King
" and country, he at leaft will applaud the cou-
" rageous efforts I have made to preferve us both
" from a crime. This leffon, my dear Florival,
" will be of advantage to you; your eyes are
" now opened to the conduct of your compa-
" nions. Still continue your regard for me; and
" never efteem me unhappy while I preferve a
" place in your friendfhip."

He fet out at day-break the next morning, accompanied by a fingle fervant. He had not gone many miles from the garrifon when he faw a large detachment of the enemy on the point of defeating an inferior number of French troops. He could not behold his countrymen in danger of being vanquifhed, without burning with ardour to affift them. Regardlefs of the danger of the attempt, he only liftened to the call of glory; and this Melcour, whofe courage his brother officers had prefumed to queftion, flew to

the

the field of battle, performed prodigies of valour, took one of the enemy's colours, and animating his countrymen by his example, they obtained the victory.

The general officer who commanded the detachment was charmed with the bravery of the young warrior, and earneftly defired to know his name. " Sir," he replied, " I will tell you who " I am directly; but, will you give me leave " firft to afk, what is the immediate deftination " of your detachment?" " It is going," faid he, " to reinforce the neighbouring garrifon," (naming that which Melcour had left,) " of which I " am to take the command." " Then, Sir," faid Melcour, " if you will permit me, I will " attend you thither, and receive there thofe " marks of your approbation that you fhall be " pleafed to honour me with."

They arrived. " Sir," faid Melcour, " the " only favour I afk of you, is to call together " the officers of the regiment of ***" (that which he had quitted); they affembled, and Melcour appeared. " Behold, gentlemen," faid he, " the unfortunate victim of a falfe ho-" nour, to which you facrifice every thing, " though it often renders you cruel and unjuft. " Becaufe I refufed to ftain my hands with the " blood of a relation younger than myfelf, and " who had expiated a very flight offence by the
" moft

" moſt unequivocal marks of ſorrow and repent-
" ance; becauſe I liſtened to the voice of re-
" ligion and humanity; becauſe I reſpected the
" laws, you have judged me unworthy to carry
" arms in the ſervice of my country. Blinded
" by prejudice, you have dared to accuſe me of
" cowardice. For that accuſation I have taken
" ample revenge. Theſe colours, taken from
" the enemy, are a ſufficient teſtimony of my
" courage." His brother officers ſurrounded
him, and embracing him, by the praiſes they
laviſhed on him, and the excuſes they made,
they atoned for the raſh ſuſpicions they had entertained of him.

The general, aſtoniſhed and charmed with
the behaviour of Melcour, preſſed him to re-
ſume his rank for the preſent, till he could have
an opportunity of reporting ſo gallant an action to
the miniſter. Melcour yielded to his ſolicita-
tions, ſeconded by thoſe of the officers of the
regiment. " Accept," ſaid the general, " that
" commiſſion you was deprived of yeſterday, as
" a tacit avowal of the injuſtice of that preju-
" dice which condemned you, and may your
" example entirely root it out!" Then turning
to the officers who furrounded him, he added:
" Let the behaviour of this virtuous young
" man teach you, for the future, not to accuſe
" the perſon of cowardice, who, obedient to
" the

"the laws of true honour, and of his country, refuses to become a murderer. Re-
nounce, gentlemen, that fatal error, which
shews you the man of true courage in him
who is not afraid to wash out an injury in
the blood of his fellow citizen: behold him
rather in the person who has greatness of soul
to be above the desire of revenge. For the
future, defer your quarrels till the day of
battle, and let the contests for superior resolution be decided in the face of the enemies of
your king and country. Or, if the insult offered you is amenable to the laws, let the
laws fix that ignominy on your adversary that
his conduct may deserve. But let your warmest praises be bestowed on Melcour, and on
those who have the magnanimity to follow
the example he has this day given us."

It is impossible to describe the transports of Florival during this affecting scene. From that moment he renounced his fatal errors, and, strictly keeping the solemn promises he had made to his friend, and profiting by his example, they both were raised to the highest stations in the army, which they filled with the greatest honour to themselves, their family, and their country.

On THOMAS DAY, Esq.

IF pensive genius ever pour'd the tear
  Of votive anguish o'er the poet's bier;
If drooping Britain ever knew to mourn
In silent sorrow o'er the patriot's urn,
Here let them weep their *Day's* untimely doom,
And hang their fairest garlands o'er his tomb;
For never poet's hand did yet consign
So pure a wreath to virtue's holy shrine;
For never patriot tri'd before to raise
His country's welfare on so firm a base;
Glory's bright form he taught her youth to see,
And bade them merit freedom to be free.
No sculptur'd marble need his worth proclaim,
No herald's founding style record his name,
For long as sense and virtue fame can give,
In his own works his deathless name shall live.

THE HISTORY OF PHILIP QUARLL.

INTRODUCTION.

THE resources of the human mind in struggling against misfortunes are never so well understood, as in situations of distress and difficulty. Nothing is so feeble, nothing so helpless, as a being that has been accustomed to subsist by the labour of others, without the least exertion. This is one of the disadvantages attending

ing a ſtate of refinement and civilization. Mankind forget the ſimple dictates of reaſon and nature, and make a thouſand pernicious indulgencies neceſſary to their ideas of happineſs. One man imagines that it is impoſſible to tranſport himſelf from place to place, without the aſſiſtance of other animals, who are to relieve him from the fatigue of uſing his own legs; another, that it is impoſſible to ſupply his hunger without a ſplendid table, covered with the productions of every climate; a third cannot ſleep unleſs upon beds of down, and in a palace. Thus are a thouſand things made neceſſary to our happineſs, which have no natural connection with it, and our lives are conſumed in the acquiſition of ſuperfluous trifles. Our vanity, ever ingenious to torment us, renders us incapable of repoſe, and prompts us to be continually making uſeleſs compariſons with all around.

Surely, in this reſpect, the uncultured Savage that inhabits the woods, and aſks no more than a ſkin to repel the winds of winter, an hut to defend him from the ſtorms, and a moderate quantity of the coarſeſt food, is happier far than we. He views the whole detail of European luxury with indifference and contempt, and prefers his native woods and plains to all the magnificence of our cities; nor would the moſt effeminate

feminate native of our capital be more mortified to inhabit the rudeſt foreſts, than he to exchange them for the endleſs reſtraints and ceremonies, which we ſubmit to in civilized ſociety. He ſleeps as found upon a bed of grafs and leaves, and gratifies his hunger as ſatisfactorily with roaſted corn, or millet, as a rich and indolent citizen can do with all the accumulated inventions of arts and manufactures. But in the entire poſſeſſion of all his bodily faculties, how great is the ſuperiority of the Savage! The inhabitant of cities, pale, feeble, and bloated, drags on a tedious exiſtence with difficulty, under the incumbrance of an hundred diſeaſes, to which his intemperance has ſubjected him. Before half his life is run out, we frequently behold him incapable of uſing his limbs, and that idleneſs, which was at firſt voluntary, becomes inevitable, from the imbecility he has contracted. In vain would the beautiful revolution of the ſeaſons attract his notice, or call him out to ſhare the common bleſſings which nature diſpenſes to all her uncorrupted offspring. Neither the care of his own neceſſary affairs, the defence of his country, nor even fears for his own perſonal ſafety, can any longer animate him to the ſmalleſt exertion; and ſhould he not be in a ſituation to buy the aſſiſtance of others, he muſt remain for ever attached to one ſpot, like a

L muſcle

muscle or an oyster. How different from this is the life of an American or a Tartar! Accustomed from his infancy to contend with dangers and difficulties, he becomes hardened against all the vicissitudes of nature, against all the attacks of fortune. Wherever the earth extends her surface, he finds a bed; the forest affords him all the shelter he demands; and he can every where procure, by his own industry, sufficient food to supply his wants. In the use of his limbs, and the full enjoyment of all his natural powers, he is not exceeded by the very beasts that fly before him. Such are all the uncivilized nations with which we were formerly acquainted; such are those which are lately added to our knowledge by modern discoveries.

But the most extraordinary instances of the exertions of human beings in difficult situations, are to be found in the lives of such men, as have been compelled by shipwreck to remain for several years on uninhabited islands. Deprived in an instant of all the advantages and support which we derive from mutual assistance, they have been obliged to call forth all the latent resources of their own minds. From a contemplation of these we are enabled to form some ideas of the wonderful powers of the human constitution, when properly stimulated to action by necessity. The following narrative, whether

whether real or fictitious, seems to be admirably adapted to the illustration of this subject, and therefore we shall make no apology for reprinting it in this collection.

THE HISTORY OF PHILIP QUARLL.

PHILIP QUARLL was an English sailor, who assisted to navigate a ship in the southern seas of America. During his voyage they were assailed by such a violent tempest, which continued, without intermission, for two days and nights, that the captain and the most experienced mariners began to despair of the safety of the ship. In this exigency, Quarll, being bold and active, took a hatchet in his hand, and ran up the shrowds, by the captain's order, to cut away the main-yard, which they could not lower; but by the time he had mounted, there came a sea which dashed the ship against a rock, and, with the violence of the motion, flung Quarll, who was astride upon the main-yard, on the top of the rock, where, having the good fortune to fall into a clift, he was secured from being washed back again into the sea and drowned, as all the rest were that belonged to the ship.

Quarll, in a dismal condition, remained the succeeding night in the clift, being continually beaten with the dashing back of the sea, and being both bruised and numbed, pulled off his cloaths

cloaths which were dripping wet, over fatigued, lays himself down on the smoothest place of the rock he could find, being quite spent with the hardship he had undergone, and slept while his cloaths were drying.

His sleep, though very profound, was not refreshing: the danger he had been lately in, so ran in his mind, that death was ever before his eyes, and constantly disturbed his rest: but nature, which wanted repose, would be supplied. Having slept a few hours, he awakes almost as much fatigued as before, and faint for want of nourishment, having taken none for thirty-six hours before: so having looked upon his cloaths, which he perceived were not quite dry, he turned the other side to the sun, and laid himself down to sleep again; but still nothing but horror entered his mind.

When he awoke, he was very much terrified with his dreams, and stared about him in a frighted manner, expecting every minute some creature to devour him; but, taking a little courage, put on his cloaths, which by this time were quite dry. He then looks about him; but alas! could see nothing but the dreadful effects of the late tempest, dead corpses, broken planks, and battered chests floating; and such sights as at once filled him with terror and grief.

Turning from those shocking objects, which presented to his eyes the dreadful death he so lately

lately had escaped, he sees on the other side the prospect of one more terrible, hunger and thirst, attended with all the miseries that can make life burthensome. Being seized with the terror of the threatening evil, he turns again towards the sea, and looking on the dead corpses, which the sea now and then drove to the rock, and back again, " Oh! that I was like one of you," said he, " past all dangers! I have shared with
" you in the terrors of death: why did I not
" also partake with you in its relief? But why
" should I complain? and have so much reason
" to be thankful! Had I been cut off, when
" the cares of saving this worthless carcase in-
" tercepted me from seeking the salvation of
" my soul, I should not have had the present
" opportunity of taking care of it." So, having returned thanks for his late deliverance, he resigns himself to Providence, on whom he fully relies; climbs up the rock, and being come to the top, sees land on the inside, bearing both trees and grass: " Heaven be praised!" said he:
" I shall not perish upon these barren rocks :" so made a shift to go down to it, the weather then being calm.

Being come to the other side of the rock, he finds at the bottom of it a narrow lake, which separated it from the land: therefore pulling off his cloaths, the water being but shallow, he wades over with them in his arms; and dreſſing himſelf, walks up a conſiderable way in the iſland, without ſeeing any human creature, or perceiving any ſign of its being inhabited, which ſtruck a great damp to his ſpirits. He walks it over and over, croſs-ways and long-ways; yet could ſee nothing but monkeys, ſtrange beaſts, birds, and fowls, ſuch as he had never ſeen before.

Having ranged himſelf weary, he ſat down under a cluſter of trees, that made an agreeable arbour. The place being pleaſant and cool, made, as it were, for repoſe, and he being ſtill very much fatigued, prompted him to lie down and ſleep, during which his mind is continually alarmed with the frightful aſpect of grim death. Sometimes he fancies himſelf ſtriving with the rolling waves, ſtretching out his arm to catch hold of a plank toſſing by; which, juſt come at, is beaten back by the roaring billows, whoſe terrible noiſe pronounces his death: at other times he thinks himſelf aſtride upon a piece of a maſt, labouring to keep himſelf on, and of a ſudden waſhed away, and ſunk down by a bulky wave; on every ſide of him men calling for help; others ſpent and paſt ſpeaking; here ſome floating that are already periſhed, and there others expiring; thus in every object ſeeing his approaching fate.

- Being awaked out of that irkſome and uneaſy ſleep, he falls into as anxious and melancholy thoughts

thoughts: "I have," said he, "escaped being drowned, but how shall I avoid starving? Here is no food for man. But why should I despair? Cannot I eat grass for a few days? by which time, Providence, which has hitherto protected me, may raise me some means to get from hence." So, being entirely resigned, he walks about to see the island, which he found surrounded with rocks, at the bottom of which there was a small lake, which was fordable in most places, so that he could with ease wade over to the rock; which he did at every side of the island, to see if he could perceive any ship, whereby he might get away: but, seeing none, and it drawing towards night, he returns, and employs the remainder of the day in looking for the most convenient place for him to pass away the approaching night; and, having fixed upon one of the highest trees, he gets up as far as he well could, fearing some wild beast might devour him if he slept below: where, having returned thanks to Heaven for his late great deliverance, he commits himself to its care; then settles, and falls to sleep, and slept till hunger waked him in the morning, having dreamt over night of abundance of victuals, which he would fain have come at, but was kept off by a cross cook, who bid him go and fish for some: to which he answered, that he was shipwrecked, and had nothing to fish withal. "Well then," said the cook to him again, "go "where thou wast like to lose thy life, and "there thou shalt find wherewithal to support "it."

Being awaked, he makes reflections upon his dream, which he imagined might proceed from the emptiness of his stomach, being customary for people to dream of victuals, when they go to bed hungry. But driven by necessity, and led by curiosity, he went to the same side of the rock he had been cast upon; where, having stood several hours without seeing shipping, or aught that might answer his dream, the air coming from the sea being pretty sharp, and he faint, having taken no manner of food for near three days, he gave over all hopes of relief. Thus submitting himself to the will of Heaven, which he supposed decreed a lingering death to punish him for his past sins, he resolves to return where he lay the night before, and there wait for his doom; but being stopped by a sudden noise which issued from a creek in the rock, not far from where he stood, he had the curiosity to go and see what occasioned it.

Being come to the place he heard the noise proceed from, he sees a fine large cod-fish near six feet long, dabbling in a hole in the rock, where the late storm had cast it.

One

One under condemnation of death, and juſt arrived at the place of execution, could not be more rejoiced at the coming of a reprieve, than he was at the ſight of this fiſh, having felt ſeveral ſick qualms, fore-runners of the death he thought he was doomed to. "Heaven be praiſ-"ed!" ſaid he, "here is ſubſiſtence for ſeveral "days."

So having taken off both his garters, he gets into the hole where the fiſh lay, and having run them through its gills, he hauls it out, and drags it after him, being heavy, and he very weak. Going along, he finds ſeveral oyſters, muſcles, and cockles, in his way, which the ſea had caſt up and down the rock; and having a knife about him, he ſat down and eat a few: ſo refreſhed himſelf, his ſpirits being exhauſted for want of food. This ſmall nutriment very much recruited his decayed ſtrength; and the thoughts of his ſupply of proviſion having diſperſed the dull ideas his late want had bred in his mind, he cheerfully takes his fiſh, which he drags with much more vigour than before; and filling his pockets with ſalt that was congealed by the ſun, which he found in the concavities of the rock, away he goes to the place where he lay the night before, in order to dreſs ſome of the codfiſh; where being come, he picks up a parcel of dry leaves, and, with his knife and a flint,

struck

struck fire and kindled them: then getting together a few sticks, made a fire presently, and broiled a slice of his fish; of which he eat so heartily, that it overcame his stomach, being grown weak with fasting. Thus sick, and out of order, he applies to the recourse of the feeble, which was lying down; and having much fatigued and harrassed himself with hauling the heavy fish up and down the rock, he fell asleep until the next morning.

Having slept quietly the remainder of the night, he awoke in the morning pretty fresh and hearty, but anxious about his future destiny; for though he might for awhile subsist upon fish, wherewith he might be supplied by the sea, yet he could not imagine which way he could be furnished with cloaths and bed against the winter; for want of which he must miserably perish with cold, unless supplied by some such dismal accident as exposed him to the want thereof, which he heartily wishes and prays may never happen.

Having made these considerations, he, on his knees, returns kind Providence his hearty thanks for all its mercies that had been extended to him; begging the continuance of its assistance. Then, watching the opportunity of getting away from that melancholy place, he goes to the other

other fide of the rock, to try if he could perceive any fhipping in fight.

The wind being pretty high, fed his hopes, that each fucceeding hour would gratify his wifhing look with that object the preceding could not bring forth; but he was difappointed. The night approaching, kept back all probability for that time; however, depending on better fuccefs the next day, he returns whence he came; and being hungry, makes a fire, and broils another flice of the fifh, then lays the reft upon broad green leaves, and ftrews falt thereon, to keep it from fpoiling, and then goes to reft; and as he lay undifturbed the night before under the trees, and much more eafy than at top, he ventured again, committing himfelf to the care of Providence.

He flept in fafety that night, but with the returning morning all his anxieties were renewed, and he determined to lofe no time in providing as well as he could for all his neceffities. Accordingly, firft he begins to think of making himfelf an houfe to preferve him from the injuries of the weather; but having nothing to make it of, nor any inftrument but a knife, which could be of little fervice to him, he refolves to go to that part of the rock where he was fhipwrecked, to fee if he could difcover any thing among the wreck that might be ferviceable

able to him: and therefore takes a branch of a tree along with him, and coming to the place, he ſtrips himſelf, and goes into the water, (the water being low, diſcovering the tops of ſeveral ſharp pointed rocks) and gropes along with his ſtaff for ſure footing, wading as high as his chin, diving to the bottom frequently, and feeling about with his hands. This he continued doing for almoſt two hours, but to no purpoſe, not daring to go out of his depth; for he well knew that he could do little good there, becauſe he could diſcover no part of the ſhip, not ſo much as the maſt, or any of the rigging, but fancied ſhe lay in ſome deep hole, where it was impoſſible to get at her.

Thus deſpairing, and fretting and teazing himſelf, he calls to mind that he had a hatchet in his hand when he was caſt away, and thought probably it might lie in that clift of the rock into which he was thrown; thither he went, and looking about, perceived ſomething like the handle of a hatchet, juſt above the ſurface of the water, at the bottom of the rock; and, going down to it, took it up; which, to his great joy, proved to be the very thing he wanted.

Having got his tool, he dreſſes himſelf, and goes on to the iſland again, intending to cut down ſome trees to make himſelf a hut; looking about, therefore, for the propereſt plants, and

and taking notice of a fort of trees, whofe branches, bending to the ground, took root and became a plant, he thought they might be the fitteſt for this purpofe, and cut a fufficient parcel of them to make his barrack; which was full bufinefs for him that day.

The next morning, having paid his ufual devotion, he walks out again to look for a pleafant and convenient place to make his hut or barrack upon. He walked feveral hours, and could find none more fheltered from the cold winds than that where he already lay, being in the middle of the ifland, well fenced on the north and eaſt fides with trees, which ſtood very thick. The place being fixed upon, he hews down fome trees that grew in his way, and clears a fpot of ground about twelve feet fquare, leaving one tree ſtanding at each corner; and, with the young plants he provided the day before, filled the diftance between quite round, fetting them about fix inches afunder, leaving a larger vacancy for the door. His inclofure being made, he bends the branches at the top from both fides, and weaves them acrofs one another, making a cover to it, which being fomething too thin, he laid other branches over, till they were grown thicker. Having finifhed the top, he goes about clofing the fides; for which purpofe, taking large branches, he ftrips off their fmall twigs,

twigs, and weaves them between the plants, as they do for sheep pens, then made a door after the same manner.

His barrack being finished, which took him up fifteen days hard work, "Now," said he, " here is a house, but where is the furniture? " This, indeed, may keep the weather from me, " but not the cold. The ground on which I do " and must lie, is hard, and, doubtless, in the " winter, will grow damp, which, with want of " covering, may occasion agues and fevers, the " cholic and rheumatism, and twenty racking " distempers, which may cause me to repent my " having escaped a milder death."

In this great consternation and perplexity, he goes to see if he could spy any shipping riding within sight of the island. As he was walking along, full of heavy and dull thoughts, which weighed his looks to the ground, he happened to find a sort of high grass that grows but here and there, round some particular sort of trees, of which he never took notice before. " Heaven " be praised!" said he, " I have found where- " withal to keep my poor body from the ground, " whilst I am, by Providence, doomed to remain " here. So passes on, intending at his return to cut down a sufficient quantity of it to make mats that might serve him instead of bed and bed-cloaths.

Having

Having looked himself almost blind, without seeing the least prospect of what he desired, he concludes upon going to cut the grass which he stood in such want of, and spread it to dry, whilst the weather was yet warm. That piece of work kept him employed the remainder of the day, and best part of the succeeding, having nothing but a pocket knife to cut withal. That work being done, wanting a tool to spread and turn his grass, he takes a branch off the next tree, which, having stript of all the small ones about it, all but part of that at the top, made a tolerable fork. Thus being equipped for hay-making, he went on with his work; and as he was at it, he saw, at some distance, several monkeys as busy as himself, scratching something out of the ground, which they eat in part upon the spot, and carried the rest to their home.

His hopes that those roots might be for his use, those creatures being naturally dainty, eating nothing but what men may, made him hasten to the place he saw them scratching at, that by the herb they bear (which they tore off) he might find out the root.

Having, by the leaves which he picked off the ground, found some of the same, he digs them up, and carried them to his barrack, where he broiled a slice of fish, and in the ashes

roasted

roasted them, which eat something like chesnuts done in the same manner.

This new found-out eatable much rejoiced him; he returned his hearty thanks to kind Providence, that had put him in a way to provide himself with bread, and that of a most delicious kind. As soon, therefore, as he had dined, he went out on purpose to dig up a good quantity; but, as he was going to the place where he had taken notice they grew pretty thick, he sees a tortoise of about a foot over, crawling before him: "Heaven be praised!" said he, " here is " what will supply me both with victuals and " utensils to dress it in;" he ran, therefore, and turned it on its back, to keep it from getting away, whilst he went for his hatchet, that he might cut the bottom shell from the top, in order to make a kettle of the deepest, and a dish of the flat part.

Being tired of cod-fish, he dresses the tortoise, an animal seldom eaten but upon extremity, the flesh thereof often giving the flux; nevertheless he ventured upon it, and liked it extremely, some part of it eating very much like veal: which at that time was a very great novelty to him, having eaten no fresh meat for a long time before.

Happening to eat of that part of the tortoise, which is the most feeding, and less hurtful, he

was

was in no wife difcompofed; but, having boiled it all, he laid by the remainder to eat now and then between his fifh.

Being provided with a boiling utenfil, he often had change, by means of thofe admirable roots fo luckily difcovered; fome of which he roafted for bread, others he boiled with falt cod. This in a great meafure mitigated his misfortune, and foftened the hardfhip he lay under; fo that feeing but little profpect of changing his prefent condition, by getting away from thence yet awhile, he thinks on means to make it as eafy as poffible whilft he remained in it; for, having projected a bed, and taking the grafs, which by that time was dry, he falls to work; and a mat being the thing concluded upon, he twifts his hay into ropes, the bignefs of his leg; then he cuts a pretty number of fticks, about two feet long, which he drives into the ground, ten in a row, and near four inches afunder, and oppofite to them fuch another row at fix or feven feet diftance from the firft, which made the length of his mat; then having faftened one end of his rope to one of the corner fticks, he brings it round the other corner ftick, and fo to the next at the other end, till he has laid his frame; then he weaves acrofs fhorter ropes of the fame, in the manner they make pallions on board with old cable ends. When he had
finifhed

finished his mat, he beat it with a long stick, which made it swell up; and the grass being of a soft cottony nature, he had a warm and easy bed to lie on.

The comfort and pleasure he found on his soft mat (being grown sore with lying on the ground for a space of a month or more) so liberally gratified him for the time and labour he had bestowed in making it, that it gave him encouragement to go about another; a covering being the next necessary wanted; for though the weather was as yet pretty warm, and he in a great measure seasoned by the hardship he had gone through; yet the winter approaching, and the present season being still favourable for him to make provision against it, he goes and cuts more grass, which being made ready for use, he lengthens his loom, to allow for rolling up at one end, instead of a bolster, and makes it thicker than the first, which he intends, in cold weather, shall lie upon him instead of blankets.

Being provided with the most necessary furniture he wanted, he thinks on more conveniences, resolving to make himself a table to eat his victuals upon, and a chair to sit on. Thus, having cut several sticks about four feet long, he drives them in a row a little way in the ground, then takes smaller, which he interweaves between; having made the top, he sets it upon

four

four other sticks, forky at the upper end, which he stuck in the ground at one side of his barrack, to the height of a table; this being done, he cuts four more branches, such as he judged would do best for the seat and back of a chair, which he also drove in the ground near his table; and having twisted the branches, which grew to them, with each other, from back to front, and across again, he weaves smaller between, bottoming his seat; which completes the furniture of his habitation.

That care being over, another succeeds, of a far greater moment: " Here is a dwelling," said he, " to shelter me from the weather, and a
" bed to rest this poor body of mine; but where
" is food to support it? Here I have subsisted
" near one month upon a fish, which the same
" dreadful storm, that took away forty lives, sent
" me to maintain my own. Well, since kind
" Providence has been pleased to preserve my
" life preferable to so many, who fatally perished
" in that dismal accident, I am bound, in grati-
" tude, to hold it precious; and since my fish is
" almost gone, and I am not certain of more, I
" must by degrees bring myself to live upon roots,
" which I hope will never be wanting, being the
" natural product of this island: so I must eat of
" the small remnant of my fish but now and then,
" to make it hold out longer. Dainties or plenty
" were

"were not allotted for him that was doomed to
"slavery, but labour and hard living; and, if I
"meet here the latter, Heaven be praised, I
"have escaped the worse; I can take my rest,
"and stand in no dread of any severe inspector
"or taskmaster."

Now being intirely reconciled to the state of life, Providence, on whom he fully depended, had been pleased to call him to, he resolves to make provision of those excellent roots; and with his hatchet he cuts a piece of a tree, wherewith he makes a shovel, in order to dig them up with more ease: with this instrument he went to the place where he had observed they grew thickest, which being near the monkeys quarters, they came down from off their trees in great numbers, grinning as if they would have flown at him; which made him stop awhile. He might, indeed, with the instrument in his hand, have killed several, and perhaps dispersed the rest; but would not: "Why," said he, "should I add barbarity to injustice? It is but "natural and reasonable for all creatures to "guard and defend their own: this was given "them by nature for food, which I am come to "rob them of: and since I am obliged to get of "them for my subsistence, if I am decreed to be "here another season, I will set some in a place "distant from theirs for my own use."

Having

'Having stood still a considerable time, those animals, seeing he did not go forwards, each went and scratched up for itself, afterwards retiring; giving him the opportunity to dig up a few for himself; and as he was not come to the place where they grew thick, he laid them in small heaps as he dug them up; while those fly creatures would, whilst he was digging up more, come down from the trees where they stood hid among the leaves, and steal them away; which obliged him to be contented for that time with as many as his pockets would hold, resolving to bring something next time which would contain a larger quantity; and fearing those animals, which are naturally very cunning, should dig them up, and hide them, he comes early the morning following to make his provision; and for want of a sack to put them in, he takes his jacket, which he buttons up, and ties at the sleeves; and as he had observed, that every root had abundance of little off-sets hanging at it by small fibres, he pulled off his shirt also, of which he makes another sack, to put them in.

Being naked, all but his breeches, and the day being pretty hot, he thought he had as good pull them off too, and fill them, his jacket being but short, and therefore holding but few; taking, therefore, his bundle in one arm, and having the shovel in the other hand, he goes to the place

he

he intended to do the day before; and expecting to find the same opposition as he did then, he brought with him some of the roots he had dug up the preceding day, in order to throw them amongst those animals, and so quiet them; but to his great wonder, and as great satisfaction, those creatures, which the time before had opposed him with noise and offensive motions, let him now pass by quietly, without offering to meddle with any when dug up, though he had laid them up by heaps in their way, and stood at a considerable distance from them.

This surprising reverence from those creatures set him upon deep reflections on what could be the cause thereof; whether it might not proceed from the proximity of their shape and his: "but, then," said he, " my stature and colour of skin is so different from theirs, that they cannot but distinguish I am not of their kind: no, it must be a remnant of that awe, entailed by nature upon all animals, to that most noble and complete master-piece of the creation, called Man, which, now appearing in the state he was first created in, and undisguised by cloaths, renews an image of that respect he has forfeited by his fatal transgression, which ever since obliged him to hide the beauty of his fabric under a gaudy disguise, which often renders him ridiculous to the rest of mankind, and generally obnoxious to all

all other creatures; making a pride of what he ought to be afhamed of. Well, adds he, fince my cloaths bred the antipathy, I will remove that caufe, which will fuit both the nature of thofe animals, and my own circumftances." From that time he refolves to go naked, till the hardnefs of the weather obliged him to put fomething on.

Having picked up a fufficient quantity of offfets to ftock about two acres of land, he returns home, leaving behind him a confiderable number of roots dug up for thofe poor animals which attended him all the time he was at work, without offering to touch one till he was gone.

Being come home, he fixes upon a fpot of ground near his habitation, and digs it up as well as he could with his wooden inftrument, in order to fow his feed; which having compaffed in about twenty days, he implores a bleffing upon his labour, and leaves it to time to bring it forth. Thus having finifhed the moft neceffary work about his barrack, he refolves to take a more particular view of the ifland, which till then he had not time to do; and taking a long ftaff in his hand, he walks to the lake, which parts the land from the rock, and goes along the fide of it quite round the ifland, finding all the way new fubjects of admiration: on the left hand ftood a rampart made of one folid ftone, adorned by nature

ture with various forms and shapes, beyond the power of art to imitate; some parts challenging a likeness to a city, and clusters of houses, with here and there a high steeple standing above the other buildings; another place claiming a near resemblance to a distant squadron of men of war in a line of battle: farther, it bears comparison with the dull remains of some sumptuous edifice, ruined by the often repeated shocks of time, inciting the beholders to condolence for the loss of its former beauty.

At some distance from thence the prospect of a demolished city is represented to the sight; in another place large stones, like small mountains, laid, as it were, a-top of one another, impress the mind with an idea of the tower of Babel; and on the right hand a most pleasant land covered with beautiful green grass, like chamomile, and here and there a cluster of trees, composing most agreeable groves, amongst a vast number of fine lofty trees of divers heights and shapes, which stood more distant, whose irregularity added to the delightfulness of the place.

As he was a walking on, admiring all these wonderful works of nature, having caught cold (not being used to go naked), he happened to sneeze opposite to a place in the rock, which hollowed in after the manner of the inside of some cathedral, and was answered by a multitude

tude of different voices issuing from that place. The agreeableness of the surprize induced him to rouse those echoes a second time, by giving a loud hem; which was, like his sneezing, repeated in different tones, but all very harmonious; again he hem'd, and was so delighted with the repetition, that he could have spent hours in the hearing of it. " But why should I," said he, " waste those melodious sounds, so fit to relate " the Almighty's wonderful works, and set forth " his praise?" Immediately he sang several psalms and hymns with as much emulation and devotion, as if he had been in company with numbers of skilful and celebrated choristers.

Having spent a considerable time there with much pleasure, he proceeds in his walk, being resolved to make that his place of worship for the future, and attend it twice a day constantly.

About three or four hundred paces farther, having turned on the other side of a jetting out part of the rock, he was stopt a second time by another surprizing product of nature; a large stone, growing out of the rock, advancing quite over the lake at the bottom of it, representing something of a human shape, out of the breast whereof issued a fountain of exceeding clear water, as sweet as milk, and, when looked at fronting, was like an antique piece of architecture, which in old times they built over particular springs;

springs; and on the other side appeared as if springing from the nostrils of a sea horse. These three so very different and yet rightly compared likenesses, being offered by one and the same unaltered object, made him curious to examine what parts of every resemblance helped to make the others; and having spent a considerable time in the examination, he found every thing, which the front had likeness of, was employed in making the side representation, by being in some places shortened, and others lengthened, according to the point of sight.

Being satisfied about that subject, he enters upon another as puzzling: the bason in which the fountain ran, which was about five yards distant from whence the water did spring, being but about nine feet over every way, without any visible place to evacuate its over complement, and yet keeping the same height, without dashing or running over, altho' the stream that fell into it ran as big as his wrist. Having a long time searched into the cause, without any satisfaction, he conjectures it must make its way out somewhere under ground; so went on, till he came to the place he had begun his march at, which ended that day's work.

Having been round the island, which, to the best of his judgment, was about ten or eleven miles in circumference, of an oblong form, going

in

in and out in several places, extending from north to south, the south end near twice as broad as the opposite; he resolves to employ the next day in viewing the inside.

So the next morning he walks along the land, which he found very level, covered with a delightful green grass, and adorned with trees of divers sorts, shapes, and height, inhabited with several sorts of curious singing birds, of various colours and notes, which entertained him with their melodious harmony. In some places stood a cluster of trees, composing agreeable and delightful groves, proceeding from only one main body, whose lower branches, being come to a certain length, applied to the earth for immediate nourishment, as it were, to ease the old stem that produced them; and so became a plant, and did the same.

Having for some time admired the agreeableness and curiosity of the plant, by which nature seemed to give human kind instructions; and looking about, if perchance he could find any thing in his way for his own proper use, he took along with him a sample of every different herb he thought might be eatable. Crossing the island in several places, he came to a most delightful pond, about two hundred yards in length, and one hundred and fifty wide, with fine trees spreading their branchy limbs over its brink, which

which was furrounded with a beautiful bank, covered with divers kinds of flowers and herbs, fo naturally intermixed, which completed it in ornament and conveniency, as though intended by nature for more than mortal's ufe.

Having walked feveral times round it with much pleafure, he fat down a while upon its bank, to admire the clearnefs of the water, through which, to his great comfort, he faw many different forts of fifh, of various fizes, fhapes and colours. " Heaven be praifed!" faid he, " here is a ftock of frefh water fifh to " fupply me with food, if the fea fhould fail me."

Being fufficiently diverted with their chafing one another, which were of many beautiful and different colours, and a moft delightful fcene, he proceeds in his walk, and goes to the fouth of the ifland, where he finds another fubject of admiration, a noble and fpacious wood, whofe fhades feemed to be made for the abode of peace and pleafure. He walked round it with much delight, which made the time feem fhort; yet he could guefs it to be no lefs than two miles about.

Having viewed the outfide, whofe extraordinary agreeablenefs incited in him an unfurmountable defire to get into it, but where he was afraid to venture, left there might be deftructive creatures; yet, having recommended
himfelf

himself to the care of Providence, he ventured into it, finding several pleasant walks, some straight, edged with lofty trees, as though planted for pleasure; others crooked and winding, bordered with a thick hedge of pimentoes, which cast a most fragrant smell; here and there a large cluster of bushes and dwarf trees, wherein sheltered several different kinds of wild beasts and fowls: " Sure," said he, " this island never
" was intended by nature to lie waste, but ra-
" ther reserved to be the happy abode of some,
" for whom Heaven had a peculiar blessing in
" store. Here is every thing sufficient, not only
" for the support, but also for the pleasure of
" life: Heaven make me thankful, that I am
" the happy inhabitant of so blessed a land!"

Being hungry, and tired with walking, he goes home in order to get some victuals, and having made a fire, he boils a slice of his salt fish with some roots, and then the herbs he brought with him, which proved of divers tastes, and all excellent; some eating like artichoaks, others like asparagus and spinach. " Now," said he, " what can I wish for more! " Here I possess a plenti-
" ful land, which produces both flesh and fish;
" bears excellent greens and roots, and affords
" the best of water, which by nature was or-
" dained for man's drink. Pomp and greatness
" are but pageantry, which oftentimes prove

" more prejudicial to the actor, than diverting
" to the beholder; eafe and indulgence are apt
" to breed the gout, and various diſtempers,
" which make the rich more wretched than the
" poor; now thefe evils, thanks to my Maker!
" I ſtand in no danger of, having but what is
" ſufficient, which never can do any harm."

Thus thoroughly eafy in his mind, he propoſes to ſpend the afternoon at the outfide of the rock, in viewing the fea, and looking for oyſters; fo takes in his hand his long ſtaff to grapple in holes; and his breeches, which he ties at the knees, to bring them in. Being come to a place of the rock he never had been at before, he fees at a diſtance fomething like linen hanging upon it, which, when he came at, he found to be the main-fail of a ſhip, with a piece of the yard faſtened to it: " Alas!" faid he, " a difmal
" token of infatiable ambition! which makes
" men often lofe their lives in feeking what they
" feldom find; and, if they ever do, 'tis com-
" monly attended with a world of care. Happy
" is he who limits his defires to his ability, af-
" piring not above his reach, and is contented
" with what nature requires." Then he falls a ripping the ſheet from the yard, which he finds in one place tied with one of his garters, (having himfelf made ufe of it for want of another ſtring) " Heaven be praifed!" faid he, " this is
" no

"no effect of another shipwreck, but a fragment
" of the unfortunate ship, whose loss was my
" redemption;" which reflection made him shed
tears.

Having ripped the sail in pieces, he rolls them
in such bundles as he could conveniently carry,
and lays them down till he had got a few oysters,
proceeding to grope in holes with his stick as he
went on.

About forty paces farther, he finds a chest in
the clift of the rock, which had been washed up
there by the violence of the late storm: " Hea-
" ven!" said he, " more fatal effects of fate's
" cruelty and man's temerity! Was the sea
" made for man to travel on? Is there not land
" enough for his rambling mind to rove? Must
" he hunt after dangers, and put death to defi-
" ance? What is the owner of this the better
" for it now? Or who can be the better in a place
" so remote, and the access to it so difficult? be-
" ing not to be approached but on the wings of
" Providence, and over the back of death! Now,
" was this full of massy gold, or yet richer things,
" I thank my God, I am above the use of it; yet
" I'll take it home: it was sent hither by Provi-
" dence, perhaps for the relief of some ne-
" cessitated and destitute." Then going to lift it,
he could not; therefore was obliged to fetch his
hatchet to beat it open, that he might take away

what

what was in it by degrees. Having taken as much of the fail cloth as he could conveniently carry, with the few oyfters he had got, he went home and fetched the tool, wherewith he wrenched the cheft open, from which he took a fuit of cloaths and fome wearing linen: "Thefe," faid he, "neither the owner nor I want;" fo laid them down; the next thing he took out was a roll of feveral fheets of parchment, being blank indentures and leafes: "Thefe," faid he, "are inftruments of the law, and often applied "to injuftice; but I'll alter their mifchievous "properties, and make them records of Hea- "ven's mercies, and Providence's wonderful "liberality to me; fo, inftead of being the ruin "of fome, they may chance to be the reclaim- "ing of others." At the bottom of the cheft lay a runlet of brandy, a Chefhire cheefe, a lea- ther bottle full of ink, with a parcel of pens, and a penknife: "As for thefe," faid he, "they "are of ufe; the pens, ink, and parchment "have equipped me to keep a journal, which "will divert and pafs away a few anxious hours: "as for the cheefe and brandy, they will but "caufe me new cares: before I had them, I "wanted them not; now, the benefit and com- "fort I fhall find in them, when gone, will "make me hanker after them more; I wifh I "had ftill been without them; but now they

"are

" are here, it would be a fin to let them be
" loft. I'll take them home, and only ufe them
" at my need; which will both make them hold
" out the longer, and me grow lefs fond of
" them."

So, by degrees, he takes home the cheft, and what was in it; and now having materials to begin his journal, he immediately fell to work, that for want of other books, he might, at his leifure, perufe his paft tranfactions, and the many mercies he had received from Heaven; and that, after his deceafe, whoever is directed thither by Providence, upon reading his wonderful efcapes in the greateft of dangers; his miraculous living, when remote from human affiftance; in the extremity, might not defpair. Thus he begins from his being eight years old (as well as he can remember, he heard an old aunt of his fay) to the day of his being caft away, being then twenty-eight years of age, refolving to continue it to his death.

He now refolves to make provifion againft winter, and the feafon being pretty far advanced, he gathers a good ftore of fuel and roots, begins to line the outfide of his barrack with a wall of turf, and lays the fame at top, to keep out the wet. And as he now and then found fmall fhell-fifh and oyfters upon the rock, he makes a bridge over the lake, which in warm weather he used to wade, that in the winter he might go over dry. So, having completed his bridge, which was made of two strong poles, which reached from the land to the rock, and several lesser branches laid across pretty close, he retires home, the day being far spent. The following night there arose a violent storm, attended with dreadful claps of thunder, which the many echoes from the rock rendered more terrible; and lightnings, flashing in a most frightful manner, succeeding each other, before the preceding was well out of the sky, which put poor lonesome Quarll in such a consternation, that notwithstanding his reliance on Heaven's protection, he would have given the world (had it been in his possession) to have been within the reach of human assistance; or at least to have some company; solitude adding much to his terror and affliction.

The glorious rising of the next morning's sun having laid the mortifying rage of the blustering winds, Quarll, whose late alarm was hardly quelled, still suspecting its most reviving rays to be terrifying glances and flashes of lightning; but having lain awhile, and hearing no noise, but that which still raged in his mind, was at last convinced the storm was over; and so gets up with a resolution to go and see if he could discern any effect of the late tempest.

Being

Being come at the other side of the rock, he saw indeed surprising objects, but not afflicting; the mischief that was done, being to the inhabitants of the sea only, a vast number of which had, by the wind, been disemented; a quantity of stately whitings, fine mackerels, large herrings, divers sizes of codlings, and several other sorts of fish, with a great number of shells, of different shapes and bignesses, lying up and down upon the rock. "Heaven be praised!" said he, "instead of damage to bewail, what thanks have "I now to return for this mighty benefit! Here "the powerful agent of mischief is, by kind "Providence, made a minister of good to me: "make me thankful! I am now provided for "all the next winter, and yet longer, by which "time I am certain to have a fresh supply."

Thus having taken up as many fish as he could hold in his arms, he carries them home, and brings his shirt, which he used instead of a sack; so, at several times, he brought away all the fish, and as many of the shells as he had occasion for; of some of which he made boilers and stewpans, of others dishes and plates: some he kept water in, and others fish in pickle; so that he was stocked with necessary vessels as well as provision.

Being very weary with often going backwards and forwards with his fish, which took up all

M 6 that

that day to bring them home, he fits down to reft himfelf; and the runlet of brandy lying by, he was tempted to take a fup, which was at that time very much wanted, his fpirits being very low; but was loth to tafte it, left he fhould grow fond of the liquor, and grieve after it when gone: fome moments were fpent before he could come to a refolution; at laft, having confidered the ufe of it, which fuited the prefent occafion, he concludes to take a dram, and to ufe it like a cordial, which it was firft intended for; but the veffel out of which he drank being at his mouth, the cordial turns to a nectar; one gulp decoys another down; fo the intended dram became a hearty draught. The pleafantnefs of the liquor made him forget its nature; fo that poor Quarll, who had, for the fpace of near three months before, drank nothing but water, was prefently overcome with the ftrength of the brandy, and fell afleep in his chair, with the runlet on his bare lap, from whence it foon fell to the ground, and, being unftopt, ran all out.

Being awaked with hunger, having flept from evening till almoft noon of another day, which he knew not whether the fucceeding or the next to it; feeing what had happened, he was forely vexed, and could have wept at the accident; but confidering the liquor which occafioned it might

might perhaps, in time, have caufed greater mifchief, he was foon reconciled to the lofs, but could not with that of the right order of the days, which having entirely forgot, hindered the going on of his journal; fo was obliged to make only a memorial. That damage being repaired, another appears of a far greater confequence; the Sunday is loft, which he had fo carefully obferved to that time: how can that be made up? " Now," faid he, " fhall I daily be in "danger of breaking the fabbath, knowing not " the day. O fatal liquor! that ever thou wert " invented to caufe fo much mifchief! But why " fhould I lay the blame upon the ufe, when it " is the abufe that does the hurt? and exclaim " againſt a thing which, being taken in modera-" tion, is of fo great a benefit, reviving a faint-" ing heart, raifing finking fpirits, warming cold " and decayed nature, and affuaging feveral " pains." So blames himfelf highly for gratifying his appetite with that wherewith he only ought to have refrefhed nature; and fince that often mifguided faculty had prompted him to commit the fault, he dedicated that day, in which he became fenfible of it, to prayers and fafting; and every feventh from that he fets apart for divine worfhip only, which he hoped would keep him from breaking the commandments for keeping holy the fabbath day: fo
went

went to the place where the echoes, in many different and melodious founds, repeated his thankfgiving to the Almighty, which he had fixed upon to pay his devotion, and there fpent the reft of the day in prayers and finging of pfalms.

The next morning, having breakfafted with fome of his ufual bread, and a flice of the cheefe he found in the cheft, he goes about curing his fifh, in order to falt them: having laid by as many for the prefent ufe as he thought he could eat whilft frefh, he improves the fair weather, to dry one part of the remainder, and keeps the reft in pickle.

The winter being near at hand, and the weather growing damp and cold, hinders him from taking his walks; fo being confined within doors, he employs his idle hours in beautifying his utenfils, which were not to be ufed on the fire; and beftowed fome pains in fcraping and polifhing the reft of his fhells, fome as fine as though they had been nakers of pearl; which made them not only more fit for their intended ufes, but alfo a great ornament to his barrack, which he fhelved round with plaited twigs after the manner of his table, and fo fet them upon it.

Thus he fpent the beft part of the winter, making no farther remarks, but that it was very fharp, attended with high winds, abundance of
hail

hail and fnow, which obliged him to make a broom to fweep it away from about his hut, which otherwife would have been damaged by it.

But fhivering winter, having exhaufted his frofty ftores, and weary with vexing nature, retired; Boreas alfo, grown faint with hard blowing, is forced to retreat into his cave; gentle Zephyrus (who till then kept up in his temperate cell) now comes forth to ufher in the blooming fpring; fo mildly flips on to inform Nature of her favourite's approach, who at the joyful news puts on her gay enamelled garb, and out of her rich wardrobe fupplies all vegetables with new vefture, to welcome the moft lovely gueft. The feathered chorifters alfo receive new ftrength; their tender lungs are repaired from the injuries the foggy and mifty air did occafion; and, thus revived, are placed on every budding tree, to grace his entrance with their harmonious notes.

Quarll alfo, whom bad weather had confined within doors a confiderable time, which had in a great meafure numbed his limbs, and dulled his fenfes, now finds himfelf quite revived: he no longer can keep within; the fair weather invites him out; the finging birds on every fide call to him; Nature itfelf fetches him out to behold her treafures.

Having with unfpeakable pleafure walked
fome

some time, diverted with the sweet melody of various singing birds, and the sight of abundance of different sorts of blossomed trees, and blooming flowers; all things within the island inspiring joy; he had the curiosity to go and view the sea; so goes over his bridge; and then, at the other side of the rock, where he finds more objects, requiring as much admiration, but affording a great deal less pleasure; vast mountains of ice, floating up and down, threatening all that came in their way.

These terrible effects of the winter, which to that time he was a stranger to, occasioned his making these reflections:

He who on billows roves, riches or wealth to gain,
Is ever in danger, and labours oft in vain;
If fortune on him smiles, giving his toil success,
Each day new cares arise, which mar his happiness.
The only treasure then worth laying up in store,
Is a contented mind which never leaves one poor;
He is not truly rich who hankers after more.

So, having returned Heaven thanks for his happy state, he creeps to the north-east side of the rock, at the foot of which lay an extraordinary large whale, which the late high wind had cast there, and died for want of water. "If "this," said he, "is all the damage that has been "done last winter, it may be borne;" so went down, and measured the length of it, which was

above

above thirty yards, and proportionable in bigness: there were shoals of small fishes swimming about it in the shallow water wherein it lay, as rejoicing at its death. "Thus," said he, "the "oppressed rejoice at a tyrant's fall. What "numbers of these have been destroyed to make "this monstrous bulk of fat! Well, happy are "they, who, like me, are under Heaven's go- "vernment only." So with his knife, which he always carried in his pocket, cuts several slices of the whale, and throws them to the small fishes, saying, "It is but just ye should at "last feed on that which so long fed on you." As oil ran, in abundance, from the places he had cut the slices out of, it vexed him to see that wasted, which might turn to good money: "But "why," said he, "should I be disturbed at it? "What use have I for any? Providence takes "none, it gives me all gratis." So goes on feeling for oysters with his staff, which he always walked with.

Having at last found a hole, where by their rattling at the bottom with his staff, he judged there might be a pretty many, he marks the place, and goes home to contrive some instrument to drag them up, being yet too cold for him to go in the water; and as he had no tool but his knife and hatchet, both improper to make a hole in a board, as requisite to make a

rake

rake, which was wanting for that purpose: he beats out the end of his chest, in which there was a knot: so having driven it out, he fastens the small end of a pole to it. Thus equipped, he went and raked up oysters, which added one dish to his ordinary, and sauce to others; yet at length his stomach growing qualmish with eating altogether fish, and drinking nothing but water withal, he wishes he could have a little flesh, which he might easily, there being animals enough in the wood apparently fit for food; but then he must deprive them of their lives, barely to make his own more easy.

Thus he debates with himself for some time, whether or no it would not be injustice for him (who only by a providential accident was brought thither to save his life) now to destroy those creatures, to whom nature has given a being, in a land out of man's reach to disturb: yet nature requires what seems to be against nature for me to grant: I am faint, and like to grow worse, the longer I abstain from flesh.

Having paused a while; "Why," said he, "should I be so scrupulous? Were not all things "created for the use of man? Now, whether it "is not worse to let a man perish, than to de-"stroy any other creature for his relief? Nature "craves it, and Providence gives it: now, not "to use it in necessity, is undervaluing the gift."

So

So having concluded upon catching some of those animals he had seen in the wood, he considers by what means, having no dogs to hunt, nor guns to shoot. Having paused a while, he resolves upon making gins, wherewith he had seen hares catched in Europe: thus taking some of the cords which he found with the sail at the outside of the rock, he goes to work, and makes several, which he fastens at divers gaps in the thickset within the wood, through which he judged that sort of beast, he had a mind for, went.

Impatient to know the success of his snares, he gets up betimes the next morning, and goes to examine them; in one he found a certain animal something like a fawn, the colour of a deer, but feet and ears like a fox, and as big as a well-grown hare. He was much rejoiced at his game, whose mouth he immediately opened, to see if he could find out whether it fed upon grass, or lived upon prey: the creature being caught by the neck, and strangled with struggling, before it died, had brought up in its throat some of the greens it had been eating, which very much pleased him; accounting those which lived upon flesh as bad as carrion.

Having returned thanks for his good luck, he takes it home in order to dress part of it for his dinner; so cases and guts it: but it proving to be a female, big with three young ones, grieved him

to

to the heart, and made him repent making thofe killing noofes. "What pity," faid he, that fo "many lives fhould be loft, and creatures wafted! "One would have ferved me four days; and here "are four killed at once. Well, henceforth, to "prevent the like evil, I will take alive what I "juft want, and fave all the females." So, having ftuck a long ftick at both ends in the ground, making a half circle, he hangs one quarter of the animal upon a ftring before a good fire, and fo roafts it.

His dinner being ready, having faid grace, he fet to eating with an uncommon appetite; and, whether it was the novelty of the difh, or that the meat did really deferve the praife, he really thought he never eat any thing of flefh, till then, comparable to it, either for tafte or tendernefs.

Having dined both plentifully and delicioufly, he moft zealoufly returns kind Providence thanks for the late, and all favours received; then purfuant to his refolution, he goes to making nets, in order to take his game alive for the future; and as he had no fmall twine to make it with, he was obliged to unravel fome of the fail which he luckily had by him; and with the thread, twifted fome of the bignefs he judged proper for that ufe.

Having made a fufficient quantity, he makes a couple of nets, about four feet fquare, which he faftens in the room of the killing fnares; fo
fo

so retired, and resolved to come and examine them every morning.

Several days passed without taking any thing, so that he wanted flesh for a whole week, which did begin to disorder his stomach, but not his temper; being entirely resigned to the will of Providence, and fully contented with whatever Heaven was pleased to send.

One afternoon, which was not his customary time of day to examine his nets, being too visible in the day time for game to run in; he happened to walk in the wood, to take the full dimensions thereof, so chanced to go by his nets; in one of which were taken two animals, as big as a kid six weeks old, of a bright dun, their horns upright and straight, their shape like a stag, most curiously limbed, a small tuft of hair on each shoulder and hip. By their horns, which were but short, they appeared to be very young, which rejoiced him the more, being in hopes to tame those which he did not want for present use; so carried them home joyful of his game, depending upon a good dinner; but was sadly disappointed: the animals he found were antelopes (calling to mind he had seen them in his travels), which proving both females, he had made a resolution to preserve. Though they were too young to be with kid, and he in great need of flesh, yet he would not kill them; so with cords

fastens

fastens them to the outside of his lodge; and with constant feeding them, in two months time made them so tame, that they followed him up and down; which added much to the pleasure he already took in his habitation, which by that time was covered with green leaves, both top and sides; the stakes it was made of having struck root, and shot out young branches, whose strength increasing that summer, to fill up the vacancy between each plant, he pulled the turfs wherewith he had covered the outside and top of the hut between them, to keep the cold out in the winter.

His former hut, being now become a pleasant arbour, gave him encouragement to bestow some pains about it towards the embellishment of it, which seemed to depend on being well attended. He resolved upon keeping it pruned and watered, the better to make it grow thick and fast, which answered his intent; for in three years time, the stems of every plant that composed the arbour, were grown quite close, and made a solid wall of about six inches thick, covered with green leaves without, which lay most regular and even, and within had a most agreeable smooth bark, of a pleasant olive colour.

His late arbour being, by his care and time, and nature's assistance, become a matchless lodge, as intended by nature for something more than human guests, he now consults to make it as commodious

ous as beautiful. "Here is," said he, "a delightful dwelling, warm in the winter, and cool in the summer; delightful to the eye, and comfortable to the body; pity it should be employed to any use but repose and delight!" So resolved upon making a kitchen near it. Thus having fixed upon a place convenient at the side of his lodge, about six feet from it, twelve in length, and eight in breadth, which he enclosed with the turfs that covered the outside of his arbour, before it was sufficiently thick to keep out the cold; then having laid sticks across the top of the walls, which were about eight feet high, he lays turf thereon, and so covers it, leaving an open place for the smoke to go out.

The outside being done, he goes about inside necessaries, as fire-places to roast and boil at; thus cuts a hole in the ground, at a small distance from the wall, after the manner of stew-stoves in noblemens' kitchens; then, at another place, he sets two flat stones, about eight or nine inches broad, and one foot long, edgeways, opposite to one another, near two feet asunder; then puts a third in the same manner, at the end of the other two; so makes a fire-place fit to roast at: then, for other conveniences, he weaves twigs about sticks, stuck in the wall on one side of the kitchen, where he lays the shells fit for utensils, which both adorned and furnished it.

Having

Having completed that piece of work, he goes and visits his plantations, which he finds in a thriving condition; the roots being, in six months time, grown from the bigness of a pea (as they were when first set) to that of an egg: his antelopes also were come to their full growth and complete beauty, which exceeded most four-footed beasts, having a majestic presence, body and limbs representing a stag, and the noble march of a horse: so every thing concurred to his happiness. For which having returned his most liberal benefactor his grateful acknowledgments, he thinks on means to prevent any obstructions that may intercept the continuation thereof; and as the want of cloaths was the only cause he could think of to make him uneasy, having but the jacket and hose which were given him on board, to save his own cloaths, which when worn out he could not recruit; therefore, to accustom himself to go without, he lessens those he had, and takes away the lining from the outside, in order to wear the thickest in the coldest weather, and so thins his dress by degrees, till at last he went quite naked.

Having thus concluded, as being the best shift necessity could raise him, he falls to ripping his jacket, in the lining whereof he finds seven peas and three beans, which were got in a hole at the corner of his pocket.

Those

Those few made him wish for more, which he had no room to hope for, they being raifed by feed, which the ifland did not produce :— " Thefe few," faid he, " which at prefent are " hardly fufficient to fatisfy a woman's longing, " may, with time and induftry, be improved to " a quantity large enough to ferve me for a " meal;" then lays them up againft a proper time to fet them; fo fpent the remainder of that fummer in walking about the ifland, watering his lodge, weeding his root plantation, attending his nets, which now and then fupplied him with an antelope or goat, to eat at intervals between fifh he commonly found on the rock after high winds and ftorms; never failing to vifit the fea three or four times a week, according as the weather did prove; thus diverting many anxious hours with variety of objects that element affords. Sometimes he had the pleafure of feeing great whales chafing one another, fpouting large ftreams of water out of their gills and noftrils; at other times, numbers of beautiful dolphins rolling amongft the waves; now and then a quantity of ftrange monftrous fifh playing on the furface of the fea, fome whereof had heads (not common to fifhes) like thofe of hogs; others not unlike thofe of dogs, calves, horfes, lions, bulls, goats, and feveral other creatures: fome chafing another fort; which to avoid being taken, would quit their element, and seek refuge in the air, and fly some yards above the water; till their fins being dry, obliged them to plunge in again.

These pastimes being generally succeeded with bad weather, and dreadful storms, checked the pleasure they gave with a dread of the evil that threatened to follow. Thus commiserating the case of those whose misfortune is to be exposed to them; having spent some time in reflection, he goes to his usual devotion, and calling to mind, that in all that time he never saw a young fish in the pond, he conjectured that something might destroy the small ones; and as he imagined so it proved: for at his approach, a large fowl flew out of the pond with a fish in its bill, being too large for it to swallow.

At that distance, the bird being also upon the wing, he could neither discern colour nor make; but he had the satisfaction of discovering the cause why the fishes did not increase, they being devoured when young by that creature; which to prevent for the future, he studies means to kill the destroyer, nets not being proper instruments; it being requisite, for that purpose, to have one all round, as also to cover the pond, which was impossible by reason of its largeness; and a less being of no use, the birds probably not coming to one certain place. He wished for a gun and ammunition fitting, as being the most probable

things

things to succeed; but no such instrument being within his reach, he ponders again; during which time, a cross-bow offers itself to his mind, but is as distant from his reach as the gun. It is true, there was stuff enough in the island to make many, but no tools but a hatchet and pocket knife, wherewith, if he made shift to cut and shape a bow, he could not make a latch and spring necessary to it; so he must not think on it: yet, a bow being the only thing he could apply to, he goes about one forthwith. Thus having picked a branch of a tree, which had the resemblance of yew, and as tough, of which they are sometimes made, he, with the tools he had, made a shift to make one about six feet long, and arrows of the same, which he hardens and straightens over the fire, then having slit them at one end, about two or three inches, he slips in a bit of parchment, cut sharp at one end, and about three inches at the other, then ties the end close, to keep it in, which served for feathers; and, with the ravelling of some of the sail, he makes a string to it.

Thus equipped for an archer, wanting nothing but skill, which is only to be gained by practice, he daily exercises shooting at a mark for the space of a fortnight; in which time he made such an improvement, that at three shoots he would hit a mark of about three inches square, at near fifty paces distance.

Being sufficiently skilled, he goes and lies in wait for his desired game; so placed himself behind a tree, as near the pond as he could, whither the bird came in a few hours after.

The creature being pitched upon the bank, never stood still, but kept running round, watching for a sizeable fish fit to swallow; so that he had no opportunity to shoot; till having, at last, espied out one, it launched itself into the pond, but rose more slowly, which gave him time to take aim: nevertheless, he missed it being in motion; but when come to the top, he struck it through the body as it opened its wings, and laid it flat on the other side of the pond. He took it up, wonderfully pleased at his good success the first time of his practising his new acquired art; yet, having taken notice of the bird's beauty, he had a regret for its death, though he might, in time, have rued its living; the flock of fish weekly decreasing, by his own catching one now and then with a small net he made for that use, when short of other provisions, and their recruiting prevented by that bird's daily devouring their young.

The inexpressible beauty of the feathers, which were after the nature of a drake, every
one

one diſtinguiſhed from another by a rim round the edge thereof, about the breadth of a large thread, and of a changeable colour, from red to aurora and green; the ribs of a delightful blue, and the feathers pearl colour, ſpeckled with a bright yellow; the breaſt and belly (if it might be ſaid to be of any particular colour) was that of a dove's feather rimmed like the back, diverſly changing; the head, which, was like that of a ſwan for make, was purple alſo, changing as it moved; the bill like burniſhed gold; eyes like a ruby, with a rim of gold round it; the feet the ſame as the bill; the ſize of the bird was between a middling gooſe and a duck, and in ſhape reſembling a ſwan.

Having bemoaned the death of that delightful creature, he carefully takes out its fleſh, which, corrupting, would ſpoil the outſide; then fills the ſkin with ſweet herbs, which he dried for that uſe; and having ſewed up the place he had cut open to take the fleſh out, he ſet it up in his lodge.

His good ſuccefs in archery made him love the exerciſe; ſo that what odd hours he had in the day (beſides thoſe he ſet apart for his divine worſhip, and thoſe neceſſary occupations about his lodge, plantations, and making remarks) he beſtowed in ſhooting at the mark, which in time made him ſo expert, that he hardly would miſs a ſtand-a standing mark the bigness of a dove, at forty or fifty yards distance, once in ten times; and would shoot tolerably well flying, having once occasion to try it upon a monstrous eagle, which often flew round over the place where his antelopes and goats fed, near his lodge, which he shot at, fearing it would damage them, and killed it with the second arrow.

The summer being over, during which, having been much taken up about his habitation and plantations, he had neither time nor opportunity to make remarks, farther than it was some days very showery, and for the most part generally very hot; but now the weather being grown something cold, and the wind pretty sharp, he must be obliged to put on some cloaths to keep it off, being as yet too tender to go any longer without; next to provide for his antelopes against the approaching winter; so makes a lodge for them, at the backside of his kitchen, with sticks, which he drove into the ground, about two feet from the wall, and then bends them about three feet from the ground, and sticks them in the said wall, and smaller branches he interwove between them: he shuts up the front, and covers the top, leaving both ends open for the antelopes to go in at; then lays grass (which he dried on purpose) in the said lodge, for them to lie on. Thus, having dug up a cona confiderable quantity of roots, and being already ftocked with falt-fifh, both dry and in pickle, he was pretty well provided for his cattle and himfelf, againft the enfuing winter, which proved much like the preceding one, only not fo ftormy.

The fucceeding fpring having awaked flumbering nature, and revived what the preceding hard feafon had caufed to droop, every vegetable puts on new cloathing and recovers its wonted beauty; each animal affumes frefh vigour; the beafts in the wood leap and bound for joy, and each bird on the trees fings for gladnefs. The whole creation is, as it were, repaired, and every creature decked with new life. Love by Nature's direction, for the increafe of every kind, warms their harmlefs breafts; each animal feeks a mate; our tame antelopes quit their abode, and range the woods for the relief ordained to quell their innocent paffion; which being affuaged, they return home, pregnant with young, to their mafter's great fatisfaction; who, having given them over, was doubly rejoiced to fee them come again in an increafing condition. "Heaven be praifed!" faid he, "I fhall have a " ftock of my own, and will not fear wanting."

So, having made fitting preparations againft their kidding, he goes and examines the improvement of his new plantation, where he found

found his roots grown full as large as any of those that grew wild. "Make me thankful!" said he, "I am now provided with all necessary "food. I shall no more need to rob those poor "creatures of that which Nature had provided "for their own proper use." Next he goes and views his small stock of peas and beans, which he found in a very promising case. So, whilst the weather was fair, he falls to clearing a spot of ground to set them in, as they increased.

Turning up the ground he found several sorts of roots that looked to bee a table, some whereof were as big as a large carrot, others less. He broke a bit of every one, some of which breaking short, and being not stringy, he judged they must be eatable; then he smells them, and finding the scent not disagreeable, he tastes them. Some were sweetish, others sharp and hot, like horse-radish; and those he proposes to use instead of spice. "Sure," said he, "these being of a "pleasant scent and favour, cannot be offensive "to nature." So having manured his ground, he takes a sample of every root which he judged eatable, and boils them, as the surest way to experience their goodness.

Most of them proved not only passable good, but extraordinary; some eating like parsnips, others almost like carrots, but rather more agreeable; some like beets and turnips; every one

in

in their several kinds, as good as ever he eat in England, but of different colours and make; some being bluish, others black, some red, and some yellow. These though not wanted, having sufficient to gratify a nicer taste than his, were, nevertheless, extremely welcome, being somewhat like his native country fare and product. So having returned thanks for this most agreeable addition to his ordinary, he sets a mark to every herb which those roots bore, in order to get some of the seed to sow in a ground he would prepare: so, being provided with flesh, fish, herbs, and several sorts of roots, he goes and examines what improvement his peas and beans have made, which he found increased to admiration; the seven peas having produced one thousand, and the three beans one hundred: having returned thanks for that vast increase, he lays them by, in order to set them at a proper season, as he had done the year before.

By this time his antelopes had kidded, one of them having brought three young ones, and the second two. This vast addition to his provisions very much rejoiced him, being sure now not to want flesh at his need, which before he was in danger of, finding but seldom any thing in his net; so makes account to live upon two of the young bucks whilst they lasted, killing one as soon as fit for meat, and so now and then ano-

ther, faving only five to breed; one whereof
fhould be a mate to keep the females from the
wood; left at one time or other they fhould ſtay
away for good and all.

The old ones being well fed, as he always
took care to do, providing for them ſtore of thoſe
greens he knew they loved; as alſo boiled roots
for them now and then, of which they are very
fond; the young ones throve apace, and grew
very fat: ſo that in three weeks time they were
large and fit to eat. He killed one; which being roaſted, proved to be more delicious than
any houſe-lamb, fucking pig, young fawn, or
any other fuckling whatever.

Having lived upon that, with now and then a
little fiſh, about one month, which was as long
as he could keep it eatable, having dreſſed it at
two different times, five days interval; eating
the cold remains in ſeveral manners; reſerving
one of the other two males for a time he fhould
be ſcanted, and in want of fleſh; but was unluckily diſappointed by a parcel of large eagles,
which flying one morning over the place where
the young antelopes were playing, being of a
gay, as well as active difpoſition, launched themſelves with precipitation upon the male he re-
ſerved for time of need, and one of the females
which he kept for breed: ſeeing his beloved di-
verters carrying away by thoſe birds of prey, he
runs

runs in for his bow, but came too late with it, the eagles being gone.

Having loft his two dear antelopes, efpecially the female, having doomed the male for his own eating, he hardly could forbear weeping to think of their being cruelly torn to pieces by thofe ravenous creatures: thus having for fome time lamented the lofs, and bewailed their hard fate, he thinks on means to prevent the like evil for the time to come ; and as his bow was not always at hand, he refolves upon making a net, and faftens it between the trees he faw them come in at.

The fuccceding winter proving very wet and windy, gave him but little invitation to take his ufual walks; fo having every thing he had occafion for at hand, he kept clofe to his net making; for which having twine to twift, and thread to ravel out, to make the faid twine, kept him employed till the following fpring, which came on apace.

Having finifhed his net, and every thing which belonged to it, he goes and faftens it to the trees, as he had propofed; then takes a walk to his new plantations, which he found in a thriving condition ; for which, and other benefits already received, he refolves, as in duty bound, to attend at his ufual place of worfhip, and fing thankfgiving pfalms, which the hardness of the weather had kept him from all the late winter; but it now coming into his mind, that whilst he was at his devotion, returning thanks for the fair prospect of a plentiful crop, his antelopes would break into the close, the hedge being as yet but thin, and devour the promising buds, which are the principal occasion of his devotion; this not altogether improper consideration puts a sad check to his religious intention: and though there was a vast obligation to prompt him to the performance of that part of his duty, yet he could not, with wisdom, run the hazard, out of mere devotion, to lose so promising a crop, which he should never be able to retrieve; all his stock of seed being then in grass.

As he was debating in his mind between religion and reason, whether the latter ought not to be a director to the former, he perceived his antelopes making towards the peas, to which they, doubtless, would have got in, had he not returned, and driven them another way: which accident convinced him he might find a more proper time to go about his devotion; no man being required to worship to his prejudice: so, having put off his religious duty till he had better secured his peas and beans, he cuts a parcel of branches, wherewith he stops those gaps to prevent the creatures going in; and having completed his work, he goes to his devotion, adding

to

to his ufual thankfgiving a particular collect for his luckily being in the way to prevent his being fruftrated of the blessing Heaven fo fairly promifed to beftow on his labours.

Having paid his devotion, he walks about the ifland, being all the way delighted with the birds celebrating their Maker's praife, in their different harmonious notes! " Every thing in na-
" ture," faid he, " anfwers the end of its crea-
" tion, but ungrateful man! who, ambitious to
" be wife as his Creator, only learns to make
" himfelf wretched." Thus he walks till evening, making feveral reflections on the different conditions of men, preferring his prefent ftate to that of Adam before his fall, who could not be fenfible of happinefs, having never known a reverfe; which, otherwife, he would have been more careful to prevent. Being come home and near bed-time, he firft ate his fupper, and then, having performed his cuftomary religious fervice, he goes to bed. The next morning, after paying his ufual devotion, he takes a walk to his plantations, on which he implores a continuation of the profperous condition they appear to be in; next he goes to examine his nets, in which he finds a brace of fowls like ducks, but twice as large, and exceeding beautiful: the drake (which he knew by a coloured feather on his rump) was of a fine cinnamon colour upon

his

his back, his breaſt of a mazarine blue, the belly of a deep orange, his neck green, head purple, his eyes, bill, and feet, red; every colour changing moſt agreeably as they moved. The duck was alſo very beautiful, but of quite different colours, and much paler than the drake's.

The diſappointment in catching thoſe delightful fowls, inſtead of ravenous eagles, as he had purpoſed, no ways diſpleaſed him, but he rather was rejoiced to have ſuch beautiful fowls to look at; yet it went much againſt his mind to deprive thoſe creatures of their liberty (the greateſt comfort in life) which nature took ſuch pains to adorn: " But," ſaid he, " they were created for " the uſe of man: ſo, in keeping them for my " pleaſure, they will but anſwer the end of their " creation. Their confinement ſhall be no " ſtricter than my own; they ſhall have the " whole iſland to range in." He then pinions them, puts them in the pond, and makes baſkets for them to ſhelter in, which he places in the branches of thoſe trees that hung cloſeſt to the water, taking particular care to feed them daily with roots roaſted and boiled, and the guts of the fiſh and other creatures he uſed for his own eating; which made them thrive mainly, and take to the place; ſo that they had a breed in their ſeaſon.

The five antelopes had by this time kidded, and

and brought ten young ones: his peas and beans also were wonderfully improved, having that season enough to stock the ground the year following. Thus he returned kind Providence thanks for the vast increase, and concludes to live upon the young antelopes as long as they lasted, reserving only one for suck of the old ones, to keep them in milk, of which he had taken notice they had plenty, designing to draw it daily for his own use; so that in a little time he had enough to skim for cream, which he used for sauce instead of butter, and made small cheeses of the rest. Now having a pretty store of dairy ware, he resolves to make a place to keep it in; the kitchen wherein he was obliged to lay his salt fish, (which commonly smells strong) not being a proper place for cream and milk: for which end he makes a dairy-house at the other side of his dwelling, with branches of trees, after the manner of a close arbour, and thatches it over with grass; which answering the kitchen in form and situation, made uniform wings, that added as much to the beauty as conveniency of the habitation.

Having completed his dairy, he proceeds in his resolution of making cheese, having learned the way in Holland; and for want of rennet to turn his milk, he takes some of the horse-radish seed, which, being of a hot nature, had the same effect; having curd to his mind, he seasons it to

his

his palate; then with his hatchet, he cuts a notch round in the bark of a tree, about eighteen inches in circumference; and a second in the same manner six inches below that; then flits the circle, and with his knife gently opens it, parting it from the tree: thus he makes as many hoops as he judged would contain his paste, which, being girded round with cords to keep them from opening, he fills with the said paste, and lays them by, till fit to eat.

This being done, which completed his provisions, he returns thanks for those blessings which had been so liberally bestowed on him: "Now," said he, " Heaven be praised! I exceed a prince
" in happiness: I have a habitation strong and
" lasting, a beautiful and convenient freehold,
" store of comforts, with all necessaries of life
" free cost, which I enjoy with peace and plea-
" sure uncontrouled: yet I think there is still
" something wanting to comple my happiness:
" if a partner in grief can lessen sorrow, certain-
" ly it must in delight augment pleasure. What
" objects of admiration are here concealed, and
" like a miser's treasure, hid from the world!
" If man, who was created for bliss, could have
" been completely happy alone, he would not
" have had a companion given him:" thus he walks about thoughtful till bed-time.

In that disposition he goes to bed, and soon fell asleep: the night also, being windy, added
to

to his difpofition; but his mind finds no repofe: it ftill runs heavy upon the fubject that took it up the day before, and forms ideas fuitable to his inclination; and as folitude was the motive of its being difturbed, he indulges it with the thoughts of company, dreaming that the fame of his ftation, and happy ftate of life, was fpread about the world; that it prompted a vaft number of people, from all parts, to come to it, which at laft induced feveral princes to claim a right to it; which being decided by a bloody war, a governor was fent; who laid taxes, demanded duties, raifed rents, and warns him to be gone, having fixed upon his habitation for himfelf to dwell in. Being fadly difturbed, he cries out in his fleep, "This is a great punifh-"ment for my uneafinefs: could I not be con-"tented with being lord of this ifland, without "provoking Heaven to bring me under the "power of extorting governors?"

There happening a great noife, he ftarts out of his fleep, with the thoughts of hearing a proclamation; and cries out, "Alas! it is too late "to proclaim an evil which is already come:" but, being thoroughly awake, and the noife ftill continuing, he found he had been dreaming, which very much rejoiced him; he therefore put on his cloaths, and haftens to the place he heard the noife come from.

Being

Being within forty or fifty yards thereof, he saw a number of monkeys of two different kinds; one sort squealing and fighting against the other without intermixing, but still rallying as they scattered in the scuffle. He stood some time admiring the order they kept in; and the battle still continuing as fierce as at first, he advanced to see what they fought about, for he took notice they strove very much to keep their ground.

At his approach the battle ceased; and the combatants, retiring at some distance, left the spot of ground, on which they fought, clear; whereon lay a considerable quantity of wild pomegranates, which the wind had shook off the trees the night before, and which were the occasion of their strife.

His coming having caused a truce, every one of those creatures keeping still and quiet during his stay, he resolves to use his endeavours to make a solid peace; and as that difference had arisen from the fruit there present, to which he could see no reason but that each kind had an equal right, he divides it into two equal parcels, which he lays opposite to each other towards both the parties, retiring a little way, to see whether this expedient would decide the quarrel: which answered his intent; those animals quietly coming to that share next to them and peaceably carrying it away, each to their quarters.

ters. This occasioned several reflections on the frivolous, and often unjust quarrels that arise among Princes, which create such bloody wars, as prove the destruction of vast numbers of their subjects. "If monarchs," said he, "always act-"ed with as much reason as these creatures, "how much blood and money would they "save!" Thus he goes on to his usual place of worship, in order to return thanks, that he was free of that evil, the dream whereof had so tortured his mind, though he confessed he justly deserved the reality, for his uneasiness in the happiest of circumstances.

Having paid his devotion, he takes a walk to see how his peas and beans came on, which he found in a very improving disposition, each stem bearing a vast number of well filled pods.— "Heaven be praised!" said he, "I shall eat of "this year's crop, and have sufficient to stock "my ground the ensuing one."

Thus being plentifully supplied with necessaries, and in a pleasant island, every thing about him being come to perfection; his dwelling, which seems intended by Nature for some immortal guest, being, by time, yearly repaired and improved, leaving no room for care; yet the unwise man, as if an enemy to his own ease, cannot be contented with the enjoyment of more than he could reasonably crave, but must disturb

his

his mind with what concerns him not: "What pity," said he, "so delightful a habitation, at-
"tended with such conveniencies, and situated
"in so wholesome an air, and fruitful a land,
"should at my death lose all those wonderful
"properties, being become useless for want of
"somebody to enjoy them? What admiration
"will here be lost for want of beholders? But
"what kind of man could I settle it upon, wor-
"thy of so fine an inheritance? Were it my
"pleasure to chuse myself an heir, such only ap-
"pear virtuous, whose weak nature confides to
"chastity; every constitution cannot bear ex-
"cess: want of courage occasions mildness, and
"lack of strength good temper: thus virtue is
"made a cloak to infirmity. But why do I thus
"willingly hamper myself with those cares Pro-
"vidence has been pleased to free me of?"

Thus he holds the island from Providence: freely he bequeaths it to whom Providence shall think fit to bestow it upon; and that his heir may the better know the worth of the gift, he draws a map of the whole estate, and made an inventory of every individual tenement, appurtenances, messuages, goods, and chattels, and also a draft of the terms and conditions he is to hold the here-mentioned possession upon; viz.

Imprimis, A fair and most pleasant island, richly stocked with fine trees, and adorned with
several

several delightful groves, planted and improved by Nature, stored with choice and delicious roots and plants for food, bearing peas and beans; likewise a noble fish pond, well stocked with divers sorts of curious fish; and a spacious wood, harbouring several sorts of wild fowl, and beasts, fit for a King's table.

Item, A dwelling commenced by art, improved by Nature, and completed by time, which yearly keeps it in repair, and also its furniture.

Item, The offices and appurtenances thereof, with the utensils thereunto belonging; which said island, dwelling, &c. are freehold, and clear from taxes; in no temporal dominion, therefore screened from any impositions, duties, and exactions; defended by Nature from invasions or assaults; guarded and supported by Providence: all which incomparable possessions are to be held upon the following terms, viz.

That whosoever shall be by Providence settled in this blessed abode, shall, morning and evening, constantly (unless prevented by ill weather or accident) attend at the east side of this island, and within the alcove Nature prepared for the lodgment of several harmonious echoes, and there pay his devotion, singing thanksgiving psalms to the great Origin and Director of all things, whose praises he will have the comfort to hear repeated by melodious voices.

Next,

Next, he shall religiously observe and keep a seventh day for worship only, from the rising of the sun until the going down thereof: therefore he shall, the day before, make all necessary provision for that day.

That he shall, after any tempestuous wind or storm, visit the sea at the outside of the rock, at the east, south, west, and north ends, in order to assist any one in distress.

He shall not be wasteful of any thing whatsoever, especially of any creature's life; killing no more than what is necessary for his health: but shall every day examine his nets, setting at liberty the overplus of his necessity, lest they should perish in their confinement.

He must also keep every thing in the same order and cleanness he shall find them in; till and manure the ground yearly; set and sow plants and seeds, fit for food, in their proper seasons.

Having written this at the bottom of the map he had drawn, being supper time, he takes his meal; then goes to his usual evening devotion; and, after an hour's walk, to his bed, sleeping quietly all night, as being easy in his mind.

The next morning he takes his usual walks, and visits his nets. In that he had set for eagles, he found a fowl as big as a turkey, but the colour of a pheasant, only a tail like a partridge; this having no sign of being a bird of prey, he was
loth

loth to kill it; but having had no fresh meat for above a week, he yields to his appetite, and dresses it, eating part thereof for his dinner: it was very fat and plump, and eat much like a pheasant, but rather tenderer, and fuller of gravy.

Though he was very well pleased with the bird he had taken, yet he had rather it had been one of the eagles which kept his young antelopes in jeopardy; but as he could not destroy them with his net, which had hung a considerable time without the intended success, he projects the prevention of their increase, by destroying their eggs, leaving his nets wholly for the use they had been successful in; and searches the clifts of the rocks next the sea, where those birds commonly build, where having found several nests, he takes away the eggs that were in them, being then their breeding time, and carries them home, in order to empty the shells, and hang them up and down in his habitation, amongst the green leaves which covered the cicling thereof; but having accidentally broke one, and the yolk and white thereof being like that of a turkey, he had the curiosity to boil one and taste it, which eat much after the manner of a swan's. The rest he saved to eat now and then for a change, reaping a double advantage by robbing those birds, lessening thereby
the

the damage they might do him in time, and adding a dish to his present fare.

In this prosperous way he lived fifteen years, finding no alteration in the weather or seasons, nor meeting in all the time with any transactions worthy of record; still performing his usual exercises, and taking his walks with all the content and satisfaction his happy condition could procure, entirely forsaking all thoughts and desires of ever quitting the blessed station he then had in his possession.

Thus having walked the island over and over (which though delightful, yet the frequent repetition of the wonders it produces, renders them, as it were, common, and less admirable) he proceeds to view the sea, whose fluid element being ever in motion, daily affords new objects of admiration.

The day being fair, and the weather as calm, he sat down upon the rock, taking pleasure in seeing the waves roll, and, as it were, chace one another; the next pursuing the first, on which it rides, when come at; and being itself overtaken by a succeeding, is also mounted on thus, wave upon wave, till a bulky body is composed, too heavy for the undermost to bear, and then sinks all together: this, said he, is a true emblem of ambition; men striving to outdo one another are often undone.

As

As he was making reflections on the emptiness of vanity and pride, returning Heaven thanks that he was separated from the world, which abounds in nothing else, a ship appears at a great distance, a sight he had not seen since his shipwreck: " Unlucky invention!" said he, " that thou shouldest ever come into men's " thoughts! The Ark, which gave the first notion " of a floating habitation, was ordered for the " preservation of man; but its fatal copies daily " expose him to destruction." Having therefore returned Heaven thanks for his being out of those dangers, he makes a solemn vow, never to return into them again, though it were to gain the world; but his resolution proved as brittle as his nature was frail. The men on board had spied him out with their perspective glasses; and supposing him to be shipwrecked, and to want relief, sent their long-boat with two men to fetch him away.

At their approach his heart alters its motion; his blood stops from its common course; his sinews are all relaxed, which entirely unframes his reason, and makes him a stranger to his own inclination, which, struggling with his wavering resolution, occasions a debate between hope and fear; but the boat being come pretty nigh, gave hope the advantage, and his late resolution yields to his revived inclination; which being now encouraged

couraged by a probable opportunity of being answered, rushes on to execution. He now, quitting all his former reliance on Providence, depends altogether upon his getting away, blessing the lucky opportunity of seeing his blessed country again, for which pleasure he freely quits and forsakes all the happiness he enjoyed; gladly abandoning his delightful habitation, and plentiful island. He thinks no more of Providence; his mind is entirely taken up with his voyage; but disappointment, which often attends the greatest probabilities, snatches success out of his hand before he could grasp it, and intercepts his supposed infallible retreat: the boat could not approach him, by reason of the rocks running a great way into the sea under water; nor could he come at the boat for sharp points, and deep holes, which made it unfordable as well as unnavigable; so that after several hours striving in vain on both sides to come at one another, the men, after they had striven all they could, but to no purpose, said something to him in a rage, which he understood not, and went without him, more wretched now than when he was first cast away. His full dependence on a retreat made him abandon all further reliance on Providence, whom then he could implore; but now, having ungratefully despised Heaven's bounties, which had been so largely bestowed on him, he has

forfeited

forfeited all hopes of affiftance from thence, and expects none from the world. Thus deftitute, and in the greateft perplexity, he cries out, " Whither fhall I now fly for help? The world " can give me none, and I dare not crave any " more from Heaven. O curfed delufion! but " rather curfed weaknefs! Why did I give way " to it? Had I not enough of the world, or was " I grown weary of being happy?" So faying, he falls a weeping: " Could I fhed a flood of " tears fufficient to wafh away my fault, or eafe " me of the remorfe it does create!"

The pains and labour he had been at in the day, climbing up and down the rock, dragging himfelf to and fro, to come at the boat, having very much bruifed his limbs; and the difappointment of his full dependence on the late promifing fuccefs, as alfo the tormenting remorfe, and heavy grief, for his finful reliance thereon, much fatiguing his mind, rendered fleep, which is ordained for the refrefhment of nature, of fmall relief to him; his thoughts are continually difturbed with frightful vifions; all his paft dangers glare at him, as if threatening their return.

Being now awaked from his difagreeable fleep, he makes a firm refolution never to endeavour to go from hence, whatever opportunity offers, though attended with ever fo great a probability of fuccefs, and profpect of gain; fully fettling his whole mind and affection on the ftate and condition Heaven has been pleafed to place him in; refolving to let nothing enter into his thoughts, but his moft grateful duty to fo great a benefactor, who has fo often and miraculoufly refcued him from death.

Thus having entirely banifhed the world out of his mind, which before often difturbed it, he limits his thoughts within the bounds of his bleffed poffeffion, which affords him more than is fufficient to make his life happy: where plenty flows on him, and pleafure attends his defires; abounding in all things that can gratify his appetite, or delight his fancy: a herd of delightful antelopes, bounding and playing about his habitation, divert him at home; and in his walks he is entertained with the harmony of divers kinds of finging-birds; every place he comes at offers him new objects for pleafure: thus all feems to concur in compleating his happinefs.

In this moft bleffed ftate he thinks himfelf as Adam before his fall, having no room for wifhes, only that every thing may continue in its prefent condition; but it cannot be expected, that fair weather, which fmiles on the earth's beauty, will not change. The fun muft go its courfe, and the feafons take their turn; which confiderations

ations muſt, for the preſent, admit ſome ſmall care: he is naked, and his tender conſtitution ſuſceptible of the cold; therefore the cloaths he was caſt away in being worn out, he is obliged to think of providing ſomething to defend his limbs from the hardneſs of the approaching winter, whilſt it was yet warm. Having conſidered what to make a wrapper of, he concludes upon uſing of the graſs he made mats of; on which he lay, being ſoft and warm, very fit for that purpoſe: of this he cuts down a ſufficient quantity, which, when ready to work, he makes ſmall twine with, and plaits it in narrow braids, which he ſews together with ſome of the ſame, and ſhapes a long looſe gown, that covered him to his heels, with a cap of the ſame.

By that time he had finiſhed his winter-garb, the weather was grown cold enough for him to put it on. The froſty ſeaſon came on apace, in which there fell ſuch a quantity of ſnow, that he was forced to make a broom, and ſweep it away from about his habitation twice a day; as alſo the path he made to the places he had occaſion to go to, toſſing the ſnow on each ſide, which before the winter was over, met at top, and covered it all the way; which obliged him to keep within doors for a conſiderable time, and melt ſnow inſtead of water; leſt, going for ſome,

some, he might chance to be buried amongst the snow.

The winter being over, and the snow diffolved, the gay spring advances apace, offering nature its usual assistance, repairing the damages the last frost had done: which joyful tidings made every thing smile. Quarll, also, finding himself revived, took his former walks, which the preceding bad weather had kept him from, though there had been no considerable storm the winter before.

He having a mind to view the sea, and being come to the outside of the north-west end of the rock, sees at the foot thereof, something like part of the body of a large hollow tree, the ends whereof were stopped with its own pitch; and the middle, which was slit open from end to end, gaping by a stick laid across.

This put him in mind of canoes, with which Indians paddle up and down their lakes and rivers: and being on that side the rock next to the island of California, he fancied some of them were come to visit this island, though not many in number; their canoes holding at most, but two men; for the generality, one only; yet, as some of these people are accounted great thieves, daily robbing one another, he hastens home to secure what he had; but it was too late;

late; they had been there already, and had taken away the cloaths he found in the cheft; which being by far too little for him, hung carelefsly on a pin behind his door. Had they been contented with that, he would not have regarded it; but they carried away fome of his curious fhells, and, what grieved him moft, the fine bird he had taken fuch pains to drefs and ftuff, and care to preferve; as alfo his bow and arrows.

Having miffed thefe things, which he much valued, he haftens to the outfide of the rock, with his long ftaff in his hand, in hopes to overtake them before they could get into their canoe; but happened to go too late, they being already got half a league from the rock. Yet they did not carry away their theft: for there arifing fome wind, it made the fea fomewhat rough, and overfet their canoe; fo that what was in it was all loft but the two Indians, who moft dexteroufly turned it on its bottom again, and with furprifing activity leaped into it, one at the one fide, and the other at the oppofite; fo that the canoe being trimmed at once, they paddled out of fight.

Having feen as much of them as he could, he walks to the north-eaft fide, in order to difcover the effect of the high wind, which happened the night before.

Being come to the outfide of the rock, he

per-

perceives something at a distance like a large chest, but having no lid on it; taking that to be the product of some late shipwreck, he grieved at the fatal accident; "How long," reflected he, "will covetousness decoy men to pursue wealth, "at the cost of their precious lives? Has not "nature provided every nation and country a "sufficiency for its inhabitants? that they will "rove on this most dangerous and boisterous "sea, which may be titled death's dominions, "many perishing therein, and not one on it be- "ing safe."

As he was bewailing their fate who he imagined had been cast away, he sees two men come down the rock, with each a bundle in his arm, who went to that which he had taken to be a chest: and, having put their load in it, pushed it away till come to deep water; then, having got in it, with a long staff, shoved it off, till they could row to a long boat that lay at some distance behind a jetting part of the rock, which screened it from his sight, as also the ship it belonged to.

The sight of this much amazed him, and made him cease condoling others supposed loss, to run home and examine his own; well knowing those bundles, he saw carried away, must needs belong to him, there being no other moveables in the island but what were in his lodge.

Being

Being come home, he finds indeed what he fuspected; thofe villains had moft facrilegioufly rifled and ranfacked his habitation, not leaving him fo much as one of the mats to keep his poor body from the ground; his winter garb alfo is gone, and what elfe they could find for their ufe.

The lofs of thofe things, which he could not do without, filled him with forrow. " Now," faid he, " I am in my firft ftate of being; naked
" I came into the world, and naked I fhall go
" out of it;" at which he fell a weeping.

Having grieved awhile, " Why," faid he,
" fhould I thus caft myfelf down! Is not Pro-
" vidence, who gave me them, able to give me
" more?" Thus, having refolved before winter to replenifh his lofs, he refts himfelf contented, and gives the ruffians evil action the beft conftruction he could. " Now I think on it," faid he, " thefe furely are the men, who, about
" twelve months fince, would charitably have
" carried me hence, but could not for want of
" neceffary implements; and now being better
" provided, came to accomplifh their hofpitable
" defign; but not finding me, fuppofing I was
" either dead or gone, took away what was here
" of no ufe; much good may what they have
" got do them, and may it be of as much ufe to
" them as it was to me." Thus walks out, in

order to cut grafs to dry, and make himfelf new bedding, and a winter garb.

Having walked about half a mile, he perceives the fame men coming towards the pond. "Hea-
"ven be praifed!" faid he, "here they be ftill.
"Now when they fee I am not gone, nor wil-
"ling to go, they will return my things, which
"they are fenfible I cannot do without," with which words he goes up to them.

By this time they had caught the two old ducks, which, being pinioned, could not fly away as the reft did. He was much vexed to fee the beft of his ftock thus taken away, yet, as he thought they were come to do him fervice, he could grudge them nothing, that would any wife gratify them for fo good an intent. But having returned them thanks for their good will, he told them he was very happy in the ifland, and had made a vow never to go out of it.

Thefe being Frenchmen, and of an employment where politenefs is of little ufe, being fifhermen, and not underftanding what he faid, only laughed in his face, and went on to the purpofe they came about: then having as many of the ducks as they could get, they proceeded towards the houfe where they had feen the antelopes, fome of which not running away at their approach, they propofed to catch hold of them.

Being come to the place where they ufed to feed,

feed, which was near the dwelling, the young ones, not being used to see any men in cloaths, nor any body but their master, presently fled; but the two old ones, which he had bred up, were so tame, that they stood still, only when the men came to them, they kept close to him, which gave the men opportunity to lay hold of them; when, notwithstanding Quarll's repeated intreaties, they tied a halter about their horns, and barbarously led them away.

Quarll was grieved to the heart to see his darlings, which he had taken such care to breed up, and which were become the principal part of his delight, following him up and down, and which, by their jumping and playing before him, often disperfed melancholy thoughts; notwithstanding all these endearing qualifications, thus hauled away: he weeps, and on his knees begs they may be left; and though they understood not his words, his actions were so expressive and moving, that had they had the humanity of cannibals, who eat one another, they would have yielded to so melting an object as the poor broken hearted Quarll was; but the inflexible boors went on, cruelly hauling and dragging the poor creatures, which, as if sensible of the barbarity of the act, looked back to their afflicted master, as craving his assistance; which, at last, so exasperated him, that he was several times

tempted

tempted to lay on the ravishers with his long staff; as often was stopt by the following consideration: " Shall I," said he, " be the destruction of my fellow creatures, to rescue out of their hands, animals of which I have an improving store left, and deprive them of their healths, and perhaps of their lives, to recover what cost me nought? Let them go with what they have, and the merit of their deed be their reward." Thus he walks about melancholy, bemoaning his poor antelopes fate, and his own misfortune: " They were used to liberty," said he, " which they now are deprived of, and for which they will pine and die, which, for their sake I cannot but wish; for life, without liberty, is a continual death."

As he was walking, thinking (as it is usual after the loss of any thing one loves) of the pleasure he had during the enjoyment, the ruffians having secured the poor animals, came back with ropes in their hands. " What do they want next?" said he, " have they not all they desire; would they carry away my habitation also? Sure they have no design on my person; if so, they will not take it so easily as they did my dear antelopes." Thus he resolved to exercise his quarter staff, if they offered to lay hands on him. The villains, whose design was to bind him, and so carry him away,

seeing

seeing him armed and resolute, did not judge it safe for them to advance within the reach of his weapon, but kept at some distance, divining how to seize him.

Quarll, who, by their consulting, guessed at their design, not thinking proper to let them come to a resolution, makes at the nearest, who immediately takes to his heels, and then to the next, who immediately does the same. Thus he follows them about for a considerable time; but they divided, in order to tire him with running, till the night approaching, and the wind rising, made them fear their retreat might be dangerous, if they deferred it; so that they went clear away: which being all he desired, he returned as soon as he saw them in the long-boat, which they rowed to their ship, that lay at anchor some distance from the rocks.

These wretches being gone, he returns Heaven thanks for his deliverance; and as his bridge had favoured their coming, he pulls it off, and only laid it over when he had a mind to view the sea, and goes home to eat a bit, having not, as yet, broken his fast. Having, therefore, eaten some of his roots and cheese, and being wearied with hunting these boors, he consults how to lie, his bed and bedding being gone, as also his winter gown, and the nights being as yet cold: however, after a small consideration, he concludes

cludes to lie in the lodge, which was left vacant by the stolen antelopes absence; whose litter being made of the same grass as his mats were, he lay both soft and warm.

Next morning having paid his usual devotion, he goes into the kitchen, in order to breakfast, and afterwards to take his customary walk. Whilst he was eating, there arose a noise in the air, as proceeding from a quantity of rooks, jackdaws, crows, and such like birds, whose common notes he was acquainted with; and as the noise approached, he had the curiosity to go and see what was the matter, but was prevented by the coming of a large fowl, which flew over his head, as he was going out; he turned back to gaze at the bird, whose beauty seized him with admiration; the pleasure of seeing so charming a creature quite put out of his mind the curiosity of looking from whence proceeded the disagreeable noise without; which ceasing as soon as the bird was sheltered, made him imagine those carrion birds had been chasing that beautiful fowl, which, seeing itself out of danger, stood still, very calm and composed; which gave him the opportunity of making a discussion of every individual beauty which composed so delightful an object; it was about the bigness and form of a swan, almost headed like it, only the bill was not so long nor so broad, and red like

like coral; his eyes like thofe of a hawk, his head of a mazarine blue, and on the top of it a tuft of fhining gold coloured feathers, which fpread over it, hanging near three inches beyond, all round; its' breaft, face, and part of its neck, milk white, curioufly fpeckled with fmall black fpots, a gold coloured circle about it; its back and neck behind of a fine crimfon, fpeckled with purple; its legs and feet the fame colour as its bill; its tail long and round, fpreading like that of a peacock, compofed of fix rows of feathers, all of different colours, which made a moft delightful mixture.

Having fpent feveral minutes in admiring the bird, he lays peas, and crumbled roots, both roafted and boiled, before it: as alfo water in a fhell, withdrawing, to give it liberty to eat and drink; and ftood peeping to fee what it would do: which, being alone, having looked about, picks a few peas, and drinks heartily; then walks towards the door in a compofed eafy manner, much like that of a cock.

Quarll, being at the outfide, was dubious whether he fhould detain him, or let him go; his affection for that admirable creature equally prompts him to both: he cannot bear the thoughts of parting with fo lovely an object, nor harbour that of depriving it of liberty, which it fo implicitly intrufted him withal. Thus, after a fmall a small pause, generosity prevails over self-pleasure; "Why should I," said he, "make the "place of its refuge its prison?" He therefore makes room for it to go, which, with a slow pace, walks out; and having looked about a little time, mounts up a considerable height; and then takes its course north-west.

There happening nothing the remainder of the year worthy of record, he employs it in his customary occupations; as pruning and watering his lodge and dairy, making his mats to lie on, as also his winter garb; every day milking his antelopes and goats; making now and then butter and cheese, attending his nets, and such like necessary employments.

The mean time, the French mariners, who, probably, got money by what they had taken from him the year before, returned, it being much about the same season; and being resolved to take him away, and all they could make any thing of, out of the island, were provided with hands and implements to accomplish their design; as ropes to bind what they could get alive, and guns to shoot what they could not come at, saws and hatchets to cut down logwood and brazil, pick-axes and shovels to dig up orris roots, and others of worth, which they imagined the island produced; likewise flat bottomed boats to tow in shallow water, where
others

others could not come; and thus by degrees to load their ship with booty: but ever watchful Providence blasted their evil projects, and confounded their devices, at the very instant they thought themselves sure of success: implements in a flat-bottomed boat were towed to the very foot of the rock, by a young fellow, who being lighter than a man, was thought fittest to go with the tools, which pretty well loaded the boat.

Their materials being landed, to their great satisfaction, the men on board embarked in two more of the same sort of boats; but were no sooner in them, than a storm arose, which dashed their slender bottom to pieces, and washed them into the sea, in which they perished, oversetting also the flat bottomed boat on shore, with the load, and the lad underneath it.

The storm being over, which lasted from about eight in the morning till almost twelve at noon, Quarll, according to his custom, went to see if he could perceive any damage done by the late tempest, and if any, distressed by it, stood in want of help.

Being at that side of the rock he used to visit, he could see nothing but a few fishes and shells the sea had left in the clifts: " If this," said he, " be all the damage that has been done, make " me thankful; it will recruit me with fresh fish " and utensils." Going to the N. W. part,
where

where he sees a battered boat, floating with the keel upwards, " This," said he, " bodes some " mischief;" but thought it not to be of any consequence. Having gone about fifty yards further, he espies a small barrel at the foot of the rock, with several planks and fragments of a ship floating with the tide: " Alas!" said he, " these are too evident proofs of a shipwreck, " to hope otherwise." As he was looking about, he hears a voice cry out, much like that of a man, at some distance, behind a part of the rock: being advanced a small matter beyond where he was, " Heaven be praised!" said he, " there is somebody, whom I am luckily come " to save, and he is most fortunately come to be " my companion: I cannot but rejoice at the " event, though I heartily grieve for the acci- " dent." Hastening to the place where he thought the cries came from, which, as he advanced, he could discern to be too shrill for a man's voice; " Certainly," said he, " this must " be some woman by the noise."

He then, with his staff, endeavoured to break that which he took to be the lid of the chest, but proved the bottom; and as he was striking, the boy underneath, calling to him to turn it up, thrust his hand under the side, which he perceiving, though he understood him not, stood still. Finding his mistake, " This," said he,

" is

"is a flat-bottomed boat, such as the French-
"men used the year before, when they came
"and plundered me. Now, am I safe if I turn
"it up? Doubtless they are come in great num-
"bers." Pausing awhile, and the lad (whom
he took to be a woman) still continuing his
moan, he was moved to compassion; and, having considered the boat could not hold any great
number, he ventures: "Let what will come on
"it, or who will be under, for the poor woman's
"sake I will relieve them; there cannot be
"many men. However I will let but one out
"at a time; if he be mischievous, I am able to
"deal with him." At this, he puts the end of
his staff where he had seen the hand, and lifts
it up about a foot from the ground. Out of the
opening immediately creeps the boy, who, on
his knees falls a begging and weeping, expecting
death every moment, as being the merited punishment for the evil purpose he came about.

Being affected with his supplications, though
the sight of the preparations made for his intended ruin had moved him to anger against that
mercenary nation, he helps the young fellow up
by the hand, and the night coming on apace,
he takes one of the hatchets that lay by, and
gave another to the boy, then falls a knocking
the boat to pieces, and directed him to do the
same, which he accordingly did.

The

The boat being demolished, they carried the boards up higher on the rock, as also the rest of the things; left, in the night, some storm should rise, which might wash them back into the sea; it being then too late to bring them away. Having done, they each of them took up what they could carry, and so went home. The young Frenchman, finding a kinder treatment than either he deserved or expected, was extraordinary submissive and tractable; which made Quarll the more kind and mild; and instead of condemning his evil attempt, he commiserated his misfortune, and in room of resentment shewed him kindness. Thus having given him of what he had to eat, he puts him to bed in his lodge, wherein he lay, till he had got his mats made up; then went to bed himself.

The next morning he rose and walked about till he thought it time for the boy to rise; he then calls him up, and takes him to the place that he usually went to every morning and evening to sing psalms; where the youth being come, and hearing so many different voices, and seeing nobody, was scared out of his wits, and took to his heels, making towards the rock as fast as he could; but as he was not acquainted with the easiest and most practicable parts thereof, Quarll had made an end of his psalm, and overtook him before he could get to the sea side, into which

which he certainly would have caſt himſelf at the fright; but Quarll, who, by the boy's ſtaring, gueſſed his diſorder, not having the benefit of the language, endeavoured to calm him by his pleaſing countenance, and prevented his drowning himſelf; but could not keep off a violent fit the fright had occaſioned, which held him ſeveral minutes.

The fit being over, he and the boy took away at divers times the remains of the boat, and what was in it, which they could not carry home the day before: then taking up two guns, "Now," ſaid he, "theſe unlucky inſtruments, "which were intended for deſtruction, ſhall be "employed for the preſervation of that they "were to deſtroy;" and taking them to his lodge, ſets them at each ſide of the door; then being dinner time, he ſtrikes a light, and ſets the boy to make a fire, whilſt he made ſome of the fiſh fit to fry, which he picked up upon the rock the evening before; then takes dripping he ſaved, when he roaſted any fleſh, to fry them with. The boy, who had lived ſome time in Holland, where they uſed much butter, ſeeing dripping employed in room thereof, thought to pleaſe his maſter in making ſome; and as he had ſeen milk and cream in the dairy arbour, wanting a churn only, there being a ſmall rundlet lying empty,

empty, he takes out one of the ends of it, in which, the next day, he beat butter.

Quarll, seeing this youth industrious, begins to fancy him, notwithstanding the aversion he had conceived for his nation, ever since the ill treatment he had received from his countrymen; and, as speech is one of the most necessary faculties to breed and maintain fellowship, he took pains to teach him English.

The lad being acute and ingenious, was soon made to understand it, and in six months capable to speak it sufficiently, so as to give his master a relation of his late coming, and to what intent. "The men," said he, "who about one year "since carried away from hence some antelopes, "with extraordinary ducks, and several rarities, "which they said belonged to a monstrous Eng- "lish Hermit, whose hair and beard covered his "whole body, having got a great deal of money "by shewing them, encouraged others to come; "whereupon several, joining together, hired a "a ship to fetch away the Hermit, and what "else they could find; therefore brought with "them tools, and guns to shoot what they could "not take alive."—"Barbarous wretches!" replied he, "to kill my dear antelopes and ducks! "Pray, what did they intend to do with me?"— "Why," said the boy, "to make a show of
"you."

" you."—" To make a fhow of me ! Sordid
" wretches! is a Chriftian then fuch a rarity
" amongft them? Well, and what were the faws
" and hatchets for?"—" To cut down your
" houfe, which they intended to make a drink-
" ing booth of."—" Oh, monftrous! what time
" and nature has been fifteen years a complet-
" ing, they would have ruined in a moment:
" well, thanks to Providence, their evil defign
" is averted. Pray, what is become of thofe
" facrilegious perfons?"—" They are all drown-
" ed," faid the boy.—"Then," replies he, " the
" Heavens are fatisfied, and I avenged: but how
" cameft thou to efcape? for thou waft with
" them."—" No," replied the youth, " I was
" upon the rock when their boat was dafhed
" againft it, and was overfet with the fame fea,
" under the flat-bottomed boat, where you
" found me."—" That was a happy overfet for
" thee. Well, is there no gratitude due to Pro-
" vidence for thy efcape?"—" Due to Provi-
" dence!" faid he, " why, I thought you had
" faved me: I am fure you let me cut."—
" Yes," replied Quarll, " but I was fent by
" Providence for that purpofe."—" That was
" kindly done too," faid the boy ; " well, when
" I fee him, I will thank him: doth he live
" hereabout ?"—" Poor ignorant creature!" replied Quarll ; " why Providence is every where.
" What!

"What! didst thou never hear of Providence? "What religion art thou of?"—"Religion!" answered the youth: "I don't know what you "mean: I am a fisherman by trade, which my "father lived by,"—"Well," said Quarll, "did "he teach thee nothing else? no prayers?"— "Prayers!" replied the lad; "why, fishermen "have no time to pray; that is for them who "have nothing else to do: poor folks must work "and get money; that is the way of our town." "Covetous wretches! Well," said he, "I "grudge them not what they possess, since it is "all the happiness they aspire at; but thou shalt "learn to pray, which will be of far more ad- "vantage to thee than work, both here and "hereafter:" from which time he begins to teach him the Lord's Prayer and the Ten Commandments, as also the principles of the Christian religion; all which instructions the youth taking readily, won his affection the more: he likewise taught him to sing psalms, which farther qualified him to be his companion in spiritual exercises as well as in temporal occupations.

Now, having company, he is obliged to enlarge his bed, the lodge being wanted for his antelopes against breeding time: he adds, therefore, to his mats. His other provisions also wanting to be augmented, and he having both tools and boards, out of the flat boat which he had

had taken to pieces, he and the lad went about making large boxes to falt flefh and fifh in; then, with the boards that were left, they made a table for his dwelling that he had before, and one for his kitchen, as alfo fhelves in the room of thofe that were made of wicker: then, having recruited his fhell utenfils that were ftolen the year before, he was completely furnifhed with all manner of conveniences; and Providence fupplying him daily with other neceffaries, there was no room left him for wifhes, but for thankfgiving, which they daily moft religioufly paid.

In this moft happy ftate they lived in peace and concord the fpace of ten years, unanimoufly doing what was to be done, as it lay in each of their ways, without relying on one another.

Quarll, who before, though alone, and deprived of fociety (the principal comfort of life) thought himfelf bleffed, now cannot exprefs his happinefs, there being none in the world to be compared to it, heartily praying he might find no alteration until death: but the young man, not having met with fo many difappointments in the world as he, had not quite withdrawn his affections from it; his mind fometimes will run upon his native country, where he has left his relations, and where he cannot help wifhing to be himfelf: thus, an opportunity offering itfelf

P one

one day, as he went to get oyfters, to make fauce for fome frefh cod-fifh which Quarll was dreffing, he faw, at a diftance, a fhip; at which his heart fell a panting; his pulfes double their motion; his blood grows warmer and warmer, till at laft, inflamed with defire of getting at it, he lays down the bag he brought to put the oyfters in, as alfo the inftrument to dredge them up with, and takes to fwimming. The men on board having efpied him out, fent their boat to take him up; fo he went away without taking leave of him he had received fo much good from; who, having waited a confiderable time, fearing fome accident would befal him, leaves his cooking, and goes to fee for him; and, being come at the place where he was to get the oyfters, he fees the bag and inftrument lie, and nobody with them. Having called feveral times without being anfwered, various racking fears tortured his mind: fometimes he doubts he is fallen in fome hole of the rock, there being many near that place where the oyfters were: he, therefore, with his ftaff, which he always carried with him when he went abroad, at the other fide of the rock, grabbled in every one round the place; and, feeling nothing, he concludes fome fea-monfter had ftolen him away, and, weeping, condemns himfelf as the caufe of this fatal accident; refolving for the future to

punifh

punish himself by denying his appetite; and only eat to support nature, and not to please his palate.

Having given over hopes of getting him again, he returns home in the greatest affliction, resolving to fast till that time the next day: but, happening to look westward, in which point the wind stood, he perceives something like a boat at a great distance; wiping the tears off his eyes, and looking stedfastly, he discovers a sail beyond it, which quite altered the motive of his former fear: "No monster," said he, "hath "devoured him; it is too plain a case, that he "has villainously left me: but what could I "expect of one who had projected such evil "against me?" So saying, he went home, and made an end of dressing his dinner; resting himself contented, being but as he was before, and rather better, since he had more conveniences and tools to till his ground and dig up his roots with. Having recommended himself to Providence, he resumes his usual works and recreations, resolving that no cares shall mar his happiness for the future, being out of the way of all those irresistible temptations with which the world abounds, to lay the best men's hopes in the dust.

Being again alone, the whole business of the house lies upon his hands; he must now prune and trim the habitation that daily harbours him, being made of fine growing plants, which yearly shoot out young branches: this makes them grow out of shape. He must also till the ground, set and gather his peas and beans in their season; milk and feed his antelopes daily; make butter and cheese at proper times; dig up his roots; fetch in fuel and water when wanted; attend his nets; go to destroy eagles nests; and every day dress his own victuals: all which necessary occupations, besides the time dedicated for morning and evening devotions, kept him wholly employed, which made his renewed solitude less irksome. And, having walked all that afternoon to divert his thoughts, admiring all the way the wonderful works of Nature, both in the surprizing rocks which surrounded the island, and in the delightful creatures and admirable plants that are in it; being weary with walking, he returns home, thanking kind Providence for settling him in so blessed a place; and in his way calls at his invisible choir, where, having sung a thanksgiving psalm, and his usual evening hymn, he goes to supper, and then to bed, with a thoroughly contented mind, which occasions pleasant dreams to entertain his thoughts.

There happening a great noise of squealing, it waked him out of his dream; and his mind being impressed with notions of war, it at first

seized

seized him with terror; but being somewhat settled, and the noise still continuing, he perceived it proceeded from the two different kinds of monkeys in the island, which were fighting for the wild pomegranates that the high wind had shaken off the trees the preceding night, which was very boisterous.

Having guessed the occasion of their debate, he rises, in order to go and quell their difference, by dividing amongst them the cause thereof. Getting up, he opens the door, at the outside of which, an old monkey of each sort were quietly waiting his levee, to entice him to come, as he once before did, and put an end to their bloody war.

He was not a little surprized to see two such inveterate enemies, who at other times never meet without fighting, at that juncture agree so well.

That most surprizing sign of reason in those brutes, which, knowing his decision would compose their comrades difference, came to implore it, put him upon these reflections: Would "Princes," said he, "be but reasonable as those "which by nature are irrational, how much "blood and money would be saved!" Having admired the uneasiness of those poor creatures, who still went a few steps forward, and then backward to him; he was in hopes to decoy one or both into his lodge, by throwing meat to them:

them: but thofe exemplary animals, hearing their fellows in trouble, had no regard to their feparate intereft, taking no notice of what he gave them; but kept walking to and again with all the tokens of uneafinefs they could exprefs; which fo moved him, that he haftened to the place, where his prefence caufed immediately a ceffation of arms, and both parties retired a confiderable diftance from each other, waiting his fharing the windfalls, which being done, they quietly took that heap which lay next each kind, and went to their different quarters.

Fourteen years more being paffed, every thing keeping its natural courfe, there happened nothing extraordinary, each fucceeding year renewing the pleafures the preceding had produced. Thunders and high winds being frequent, though not equally violent, he thought it not material to record them, or their effects, as blowing and throwing fifhes, fhells, empty veffels, battered chefts, &c. upon the rock; only tranfactions and events wonderful and uncommon; and there happened a moft furprizing one a few days after, which though of no great moment, is as worthy of record as any of far greater concern, being a wonderful effect of Providence, manifefted in a miraculous manner, though not to be faid fupernatural.

One

One morning, when he had roasted a parcel of those roots which he used to eat instead of bread, and this he commonly did once a week, they eating best when stale; having spread them on his table and chest to cool, he went out to walk, leaving his door open to let the air in.

His walk, though graced with all the agreeables Nature could adorn it with to make it delightful; a grafs carpet, embroidered with beautiful flowers, of many different colours and smells, under his feet, to tread on; before, and on each side of him, fine lofty trees, of various forms and heights, cloathed with pleasant green leaves, trimmed with rich blossoms of many colours, to divert his eye; a number of various sorts of melodious singing birds perching in their most lovely shades, as though Nature had studied to excel man's brightest imagination, and exquisiteness of art; yet all these profuseness of Nature's wonders are not sufficient to keep away or expel anxious thoughts from his mind. It runs upon his two dear antelopes, the darling heads of his present stock, which he took such care to bring up, and were so engaging, always attending him in those fine walks; adding, by their swift races, active leapings, and other uncommon diversions, to the natural pleasantness of the place; which now, by their most lamented absence, is become

P 4   a dull

a dull memorandum of the barbarous manner in which they were ravished away from him.

In these melancholy thoughts, which his lonesomeness every now and then created, he returns home, where Providence had left a remedy for his grievance; a companion, far exceeding any he ever had, waits his return, which was a beautiful monkey of the finest kind, and the most complete of the sort, as though made to manifest the unparalleled skill of Nature, and sent him by Providence to dissipate his melancholy.

Being come to his lodge, and beholding that wonderful creature, and in his own possession, at the farthest end of it, and him at the entrance thereof to oppose its flight, if offered, he is at once filled with joy and admiration: "Long," said he, "I endeavoured in vain to get one, and "would have been glad of any, though of the "worst kind, and even of the meanest of the "sort; and here kind Providence has sent me "one of an unparalleled beauty."

Having a considerable time admired the beast, which all the while stood unconcerned, now and then eating of the roots that lay before him, he shuts the door, and goes in, with a resolution of staying within all day, in order to tame him, which he hoped would be no difficult matter,
his

his difpofition being already pretty familiar, little thinking that Providence, who fent him thither, had already qualified him for the commiffion he bore; which having found out by the creature's furprifing docility, he returns his Benefactor his moft hearty thanks for that miraculous gift.

This moft wonderful animal having by its furprifing tractability and good nature, joined to its matchlefs handfomenefs, gained its mafter's love, beyond what is ufual to place on any fort of beafts; he thought himfelf doubly recompenfed for all his former loffes, efpecially for that of his late ungrateful companion, who, notwithftanding all the obligations he held from him, bafely left him at a time he might be moft helpful: and as he fancied his dear Beaufidelle (for fo he called that admirable creature) had fome fort of refemblance to the picture he framed of him, he takes it down, thinking it unjuft to bear in his fight that vile object, which could not in any wife claim a likenefs to fo worthy a creature as his beloved monkey.

One day, as this lovely animal was officiating the charge it had of its own accord taken, being gone for wood, as wont to do when wanted, he finds in his way a wild pomegranate, whofe extraordinary fize and weight had caufed it to fall off the tree: he takes it home, and then returns

for

for his faggot; in which time Quarll, wishing the goodness of the inside might answer its outward beauty, cuts it open; and, finding it of a dull lusciousness, too flat for eating, imagined it might be used with things of an acid and sharp taste; having therefore boiled some water, he puts it into a vessel, with a sort of an herb which is of taste and nature of cresses, and some of the pomegranate, letting them infuse some time, now and then stirring it; which the monkey having taken notice of, did the same: but one very hot day, happening to lay the vessel in the sun, made it turn sour.

Quarll, who very much wanted vinegar in his sauces, was well pleased with the accident, and so continued the souring of the liquor, which proving excellent, he made a five gallon vessel of it, having several which at times he found upon the rock.

Having now store of vinegar, and being a great lover of pickles, which he had learnt to make by seeing his wife, who was an extraordinary cook, and made of all sorts every year; calling to mind he had often in his walks seen something like mushrooms, he makes it his business to look for some: thus he picked up a few, of which Beaufidelle (who followed him up and down) having taken notice, immediately ranges about, and being

ing nimbler footed than his mafter, and not obliged to ftoop fo low, picked double the quantity in the fame fpace of time; fo that he foon had enough to ferve him till the next feafon.

His good fuccefs in making that fort of pickle encourages him to try another; and, having taken notice of a plant in the wood that bears a fmall green flower, which, before it is blown, looks like a caper, he gathers a few; and, their tafte and flavour being no way difagreeable, judging that, when pickled, they would be pleafant, he tries them, which, according to his mind, were full as good as the real ones; and gathers a fufficient quantity, with the help of his attendant, ftocking himfelf with two as pleafant pickles as different forts. But there is another which he admires above all: none, to his mind like the cucumber; and the ifland producing none, left him no room to hope for any; yet (as likenefs is a vaft help to imagination) if he could but find any thing, which ever fo little refembles them in make, nature, or tafte, it will pleafe his fancy: he therefore examines every kind of buds, bloffoms, and feeds; having at laft found that of a wild parfnip, which being long and narrow, almoft the bignefs and make of a pickling cucumber, green and crifp withal, full of a fmall flat feed, not unlike that of the thing he would have

it

it to be, he pickles some of them; which being of a colour, and near upon the make, he fancies them quite of the taste.

His beans being at that time large enough for the first crop, he gathers some for his dinner: the shells being tender and of a delicate green, it came into his mind, they might be made to imitate French beans: " they are," said he, " near the nature, I can make them quite of the " shape, so be they have the same savour." Accordingly he cuts them in long narrow slips, and pickles some; the other part he boils; and there being none to contradict their taste, they passed current for as good French beans as any that ever grew.

The disappointment of having something more comfortable than water to drink being retrieved by producing, in the room thereof, wherewithal to make his eatables more delicious, he proceeds in his first project; and, taking necessary care to prevent that accident which intercepted success in his first undertaking, he accomplishes his design, and makes a liquor no wise inferior to the best cyder: so that now he has both to revive and keep up his spirits, as well as to please his palate, and suit his appetite.

Having now nothing to crave or wish for, but rather all motives for content; he lies down with
a peace-

a peaceable mind, no care or fear disturbing his thoughts: his sleep is not interrupted with frightful fancies, but rather diverted with pleasant and diverting dreams; he is not startled at thunder or storms, though ever so terrible, his trust being on Providence, who at sundry times, and in various manners, has rescued him from death, though apparently unavoidable; being for above thirty years miraculously protected and maintained in a place so remote from all human help and assistance.

FINIS.

www.ingramcontent.com/pod-product-compliance
Lightning Source LLC
Chambersburg PA
CBHW021208230426
43667CB00006B/616